HERMENEUTICS

OF

AFRICAN

PHILOSOPHY

THE HERMENEUTICS OF AFRICAN PHILOSOPHY

HORIZON AND DISCOURSE

TSENAY SEREQUEBERHAN

ROUTLEDGE

NEW YORK • LONDON

Published in 1994 by

Routledge
29 West 35 Street
New York, NY 10001

Published in Great Britain by

Routledge
11 New Fetter Lane
London EC4P 4EE

Library of Congress Cataloging in Publication Data

Serequeberhan, Tsenay, 1952–
    The hermeneutics of African philosophy : horizon and discourse / Tsenay Serequeberhan.
        p.   cm.
    Includes bibliographical references and index.
    ISBN 0-415-90801-9   ISBN 0-415-90802-7 (pbk.)
    1. Philosophy, African. 2. Hermeneutics.   I. Title.
B5315.H36S47   1994
199'.6—dc20   93-40156
                                                                  CIP

British Library Cataloguing information also available.

To the Eritrean People's Liberation Front and to all those who, sacrificing life and limb, have fought for and are still fighting for the complete emancipation of the African continent. It is in light of their endurance and sacrifice that our intellectual efforts have any sense or meaning.

This book is also dedicated to the kind memory of my father Serequeberhan Gebrezgi and to my two sons, Nesim-Netssere and Awate-Hayet—to the tragic past and the hopeful future.

Contents

Acknowledgments

For unending discussions and enduring contributions not only to this study but to my intellectual development as a whole, I would like to express my gratitude to my wife and friend Nuhad Jamal. Without her assistance this book might never have seen the light of day.

For her unfailing encouragement, confidence, and a lifetime of moral example and support, my gratitude to my mother Assegedetch Aradom. I also would like to acknowledge my friend Michael Ghebreab for long discussions centered on questions of African freedom and on our beloved homeland, Eritrea.

This book, or more accurately, most of the thinking and research that constitutes its basic core, was the main chunk of my Ph.D. dissertation defended at Boston College in 1988. I therefore wish to express my thanks to my mentor, Professor Oliva Blanchette and to my two other readers, Professor William J. Richardson, S. J., and Professor Paul Breines. I am most grateful for the confidence and patience they showed me.

While it is not possible to thank everyone who has, in one way or another, assisted me in the writing of this book, I would like to thank Thomas McCarthy, Robert Gooding-Williams, Lucius Outlaw, Anthony Appiah, James Bohmann, and Reinhard Sander for helping in many and different ways.

... independence has been turned into a cage, with people looking at us from outside the bars, sometimes with charitable compassion, sometimes with glee and delight.

—Patrice Lumumba
From Lumumba's last letter to his wife,
December 1960

Introduction
Philosophy in the Present Context
of Africa

For the whole universe is interconnected; if something is
distorted, the other things connected with it suffer.
—Walda Heywat
Sixteenth-century Abyssinian philosopher

The title: *The Hermeneutics of African Philosophy: Horizon and
Discourse,* understood in its most literal and abstract sense, points to
the interpretative character of contemporary African philosophy. In
and of itself this says very little, insofar as philosophy is *ipso facto* a
specific articulation of the inherently interpretative character of human
existence as such. Thus in this introduction, as in the study as a whole,
I will progressively concretize and theoretically enunciate the sense
and character of this dry and abstract title.

As is well known the term "hermeneutics" derives from the name
Hermes, the messenger-interpreter god of ancient *Hellas.* Just as
Hermes rendered and translated the messages of the gods, so too
philosophical hermeneutics engages the sense of our mortality interior
to the limits and possibilities of this mortality itself. As Gilgamesh of
old discovered to his dismay, it is within these finite limits that the
possibilities of human life are explored and appropriated.[1] Thus, from
within the limits of this lived finitude, philosophical hermeneutics
explores the possibilities of mortal existence. In so doing it appropriates
the ancient truth of myth long lost to philosophy since the days of
Plato.[2]

Within the discourse of contemporary philosophy, this is the basic
direction and sensibility of thought opened up by Martin Heidegger's

1

Being and Time (1927) and further explored and propounded by Hans-Georg Gadamer's *Truth and Method* (1960)—the two most important figures and documents of contemporary philosophical hermeneutics. To organically appropriate and indigenize this existentially aware philosophic thesis from within the concrete historicity of post-colonial Africa is the basic task of this study.

The axiomatic point of departure for this effort is the view, first articulated by Heidegger and further developed by Gadamer, that philosophy—as, strictly speaking, with all things human—is an inherently interpretative undertaking grounded in the mortal existentiality of human existence. In this context *horizon* is the lived back-ground against which the *discourse* of philosophy is fore-grounded. Philosophy always presupposes and grounds its reflexive and reflective discourse in and on the actuality of a lived historico-cultural and political milieu—a specific horizon. Thus, the "hermeneutics of African philosophy" refers to the interpretative and reflexive presuppositional reflections grounded in and on the actuality of our post-colonial present.

To say something about the "hermeneutics of African philosophy," one at least has to explore how this discursive practice establishes itself within the horizon of post-colonial Africa. In this study, my efforts are mainly directed at doing precisely this: showing how, in progressively more concrete terms, African philosophy—even when its protagonists are not aware of it—is inherently, and cannot but be, a hermeneutic undertaking. In so doing, I will contribute my own interpretative elucidations of and to this discourse.

Properly speaking, philosophy has the peculiar characteristic of always being implicated in its own conceptions and formulations. Whether it knows it or not, philosophy, like the proverbial spider, always spins the thread of its web out of itself. It forgets this at its own peril, at the risk of being snared by its own mesh. Thus, as Drew Hyland reminds us, "every philosophic speech . . . is in part about the nature of philosophy."[3] Fully cognizant of and starting from this inescapable and fertile hermeneutic insight, what I hope to do is to explore the lived hermeneuticity or interpretative character of African philosophy in terms of the distinct concerns of our post-colonial present.

By way of an introduction then, let me begin by looking at the thematic actuality of contemporary African philosophic discourse: a discursive actuality that originates in European efforts to better and more properly colonize Africa, both physically and spiritually.

I

Starting from the mid- and late 1940s, provoked by Father Placide Temples's book *Bantu Philosophy*—published in French in 1945 and in English in 1959—there has been talk of African philosophy. As Henry Odera Oruka has observed, discussion of and on African philosophy in the 1960s was dominated by the work of this Belgian priest and his "pious" African disciples. The present prolonged and ongoing debate in and on the status, nature, and indeed the very possibility of African philosophy dates back to the early 1970s, when challenges to the ethnographic and documentary hegemony of Temples, John Mbiti, and others began to be registered.[4]

The presence or absence of philosophy in some "honorific" sense has been taken thus far by both sides of the debate as a substantiation or default of the humanity of African existence. In all of this, "philosophy" is tacitly and surreptitiously (i.e., without even the benefit of an argument) privileged as the true measure and standard of the humanity of the human *as such*. Along with this covert privileging of philosophy one also finds an obscure and rather enigmatic clash of contending political agendas—agendas which, furthermore, have not been, even to themselves and in all their consequences, explicitly declared or even articulated.

As Lucius Outlaw astutely observes, this overt and rather protracted "seemingly" disciplinary-methodological dispute is grounded on much more substantive and rather cryptic political and philosophic issues. These issues originate in the internal self-implosion of *Eurocentric* and *logocentric* philosophic thought, which is constitutive of and interior to European modernity, and on the onslaught of an African philosophic discourse aimed at redeeming the humanity of the human in colonized African existence.[5] In a nutshell, this is the existential and thematic actuality of African philosophic thought in the last quarter of the twentieth century.

To explore this situatedness in the concrete is the explicit hermeneutic task of this study. In accomplishing this, we will see that philosophy, African or otherwise, is a situated critical and systematic interpretative exploration of our lived historico-cultural actuality. In this regard it is a radically presuppositional and reflexive discourse. In our case, it is a critical and systematic reflection on the lived antecedents of contemporary African existence and thought.

This furthermore is as it should be, since the questioning of its own groundedness and originative horizon is a concern proper to and constitutive of philosophic discourse in its very nature. As Heidegger puts it:

> Reflection [i.e., philosophy] is the courage to make the truth of our own presuppositions and the realm of our own goals into the things that most deserve to be called in question.[6]

That Heidegger himself—one of the pillars of twentieth-century European thought—failed to actualize the veracity of the above statement in his own actions and political involvements does not in any way detract from the truth of the statement itself. Rather, it says something quite odious of the political *persona* of Heidegger and of the political and historico-cultural horizon of the Europe within and out of which he philosophized.

The above cannot be emphasized enough for our purposes, since we are not in any way implicated or connected with Heidegger's Eurocentric and Ger-*manic* political horizon and, in fact, are vehemently opposed to it by the very nature of our hermeneutic project. Thus, all we need to do is to note this central difference and appropriate out of the concrete actuality of our African situatedness "the courage to make the truth of our own presuppositions and the realm of our own goals into the things that most deserve to be called in question." This then is the self-assigned hermeneutic task of this study.

In this introduction I will preliminarily explore this project and in so doing map out the way that is here being outlined within the larger framework of contemporary African philosophic thought. Thus I will articulate, not only a theoretic position but also and necessarily the political and practical implications of this position. For political "neutrality" in philosophy, as in most other things, is at best a "harmless" naiveté, and at worst a pernicious subterfuge for hidden agendas.

II

The texts presently constituting African philosophy have a rather equivocal orientation. These texts focus either on documenting the world-views (i.e., the "lived" but non-articulated philosophies) of ethnic Africans or on philosophically engaging African problems and concerns. The theoretic hesitation embodied in this equivocation has been the point of contention around which the debate in contemporary

African philosophy has unfolded thus far. Needless to say, this "either/ or" is not etched or inscribed in the heavens but, thus far, this is how the debate has developed.

From the outset it is important to note that the innocuous *harmless* simplicity of this hesitation hides a bundle of vexatious and enigmatic political and philosophic concerns. This indecision vacillates around the central—theoretic and practical—question regarding the basic character of contemporary African philosophic work: Is it to be an ethnographic and antiquarian documentation of ethnic African world-views, or a systemic philosophic exploration of the problems and concerns deriving from the history and concrete actuality of present-day Africa?

In the words of Kwasi Wiredu, we have, on the one hand, a "semi-anthropological paraphrase of African traditional beliefs."[7] In stark distinction to this antiquarianism, which Paulin Hountondji has derogatorily labeled "Ethnophilosophy," we have, on the other hand, the views of: Wiredu, Hountondji, Peter Bodunrin, and Henry Odera Oruka—the self-designated school of Professional Philosophy—which, in so many words, pose a false and bland dichotomy between a supposedly "true universalistic" philosophy and the "culturally particularistic" indigenous thought of traditional Africa.[8]

In this view, Africa has thus far "innocently" been either prephilosophical or nonphilosophical. These authors who consciously label their position the "school of Professional Philosophy," with the exception of Oruka, see themselves as among the earliest pioneers of African philosophic thought. In this rather gratuitously self-flattering perspective, African philosophy is merely a "geographic designation"[9] which, properly speaking, starts with and is exclusively constituted by the work of modern Africans in philosophy or ethnography. When the latter is the case, in Hountondji's view, it is an instance of a deluded and self-deluding "philosophy" that can be written only encased between a set of double quotation marks.[10]

It is in contradistinction to the enigma of this duplicity, as Theophilus Okere points out, that the hermeneutical orientation in contemporary African philosophy constitutes itself.[11] This perspective counters itself both to the *particularistic antiquarianism* of Ethnophilosophy and to the *abstract universalism* of Professional Philosophy. It does so in an effort to think through the historicity of post-colonial "independent" Africa. In doing so, furthermore, it is fully cognizant of the fact that its own hermeneutic efforts are part of the struggle to expand and properly consummate our presently unfulfilled and paradoxical "independence."

Thus its relation to the past—tradition—is both reverent and critical.

It is reverent in that it is radically open and susceptible to that which is preserved in its own cultural heritage. On the other hand, it is critical of tradition to the extent that the cultural elements that have been preserved in it have ossified and are a concrete hinderance to the requirements of contemporary existence. This fruitful tension between esteem and criticism, when properly cultivated, constitutes the critical cutting edge of African philosophical hermeneutics.

In this respect, Kwame Gyekye's distinction and conception of "traditional African philosophy" and "modern [or, more accurately, contemporary] African philosophy"—in which the latter is constituted by its critical relation to the former, in terms and in the context of contemporary problems and concerns—is very insightful.[12] For ultimately, as Gyekye correctly points out, "philosophy is essentially a cultural phenomenon; it is part of the cultural experience and tradition of a people."[13] For us contemporary Africans, this "cultural experience" is marked and, in fundamental ways structured by our experience of and confrontation with colonialism and neocolonialism.

Thus, as Okere has demonstrated, in terms of the historicity of European thought and the contemporary discourse of African philosophy, the hermeneutics of African philosophy or African philosophical hermeneutics sees itself, on the level of theory, as the critical-reflexive appropriation and continuation of African emancipatory hopes and aspirations.[14] As Frantz Fanon pointedly observed in 1955 in the context of his native Martinique, the concrete political process of anti-colonial confrontation and political emancipation is a "metaphysical experience."[15] It is the lived historicity of this "metaphysical experience" that the hermeneutics of contemporary African philosophy makes the object of its reflexive discourse. This is also what Amilcar Cabral refers to as the "return to the source"[16] in and out of the lived context of the African liberation struggle. From what has been said thus far then, the locus of philosophic reflection and reflexivity is the concrete actuality and the phenomenal historicity of lived existence.

In contrast, what is unacceptable in both of the previous perspectives is that, in a strange sort of way, the seemingly contrary positions of Ethnophilosophy and Professional Philosophy implicitly share the "prejudice that views Africa as primitive and with a purely mythical mentality."[17] On the one hand, Ethnophilosophy does so by inadvertently valorizing essentialist stereotypical notions of Africa and Africans. The best example of this is Leopold Sedar Senghor's oft quoted remark—a standard of Ethnophilosophy—that "reason is hellenic and emotion is negro."[18] Professional Philosophy, on the other hand, is implicated in the "prejudice that views Africa as primitive" by universalizing, as ontologically normative, the specific metaphysical singularity of European modernity.

Regarding both of these seemingly "contrary" and equally unpalatable positions Marcien Towa writes:

> The danger to which African philosophy is currently exposed is that of a real blockage. The ethnophilosophers strive to occlude and replace it with their concealed credo. [On the other hand] . . . scientists [i.e., scientistically oriented philosophers] and epistemologists dismiss it overtly in the name of science or the commentary on science.[19]

He further notes that:

> The current of thought represented by P. Hountondji [i.e., Professional Philosophy] does not occlude African thought, it openly excludes it, in the name of scientificity, as not in the least pertinent.[20]

Beyond this double "blockage" by *occlusion* (Ethnophilosophy) and *exclusion* (Professional Philosophy) contemporary African philosophy is concretely oriented toward thinking the problems and concerns that arise from the lived actuality of post-colonial "independent" Africa. Thus, the situated historicity out of which it is being secreted is the essential object of its own reflexive and reflective concerns. As Towa correctly points out, philosophy is:

> The thought of the essential, the methodical and critical examination of that which, in the theoretical order or in the practical order, has or should have for humanity a supreme importance. Such is philosophy in its abstract and entirely general essence.[21]

The generality of this essence is specified by the differentiated particularity—cultural, historical, and political—within which a philosophic discourse is articulated. Philosophic discourse secures its concerns by systematically articulating the issues and probing the questions of its lived horizon. It is this situatedness itself which serves as its horizon, in and on which it is foregrounded as a discourse on its own level of theoretic abstraction.

Philosophic reflection is thus a grasping and exploring of grounding concerns aimed at the enhancement, perpetuation, or critique of its own lived actuality. In other words, and quite precisely:

one has to see that any particular philosophy is always elaborated by philosophers who are not themselves abstractions, but are beings of flesh and bones who belong to a continent, to a particular culture, and to a specific period . . . for a particular philosopher to really philosophize is necessarily to examine in a critical and methodic manner the essential problems of his milieu and of his period. He will thus elaborate a philosophy that is in an explicit or implicit relation with his times and his milieu.[22]

For *us*—contemporary Africans—the "time" and the "milieu" within which the discourse of African philosophy is elaborated is the actuality of our post-colonial enigmatic present. To think the historicity and presence of this situatedness means to concretely query the contradictions of *our* post-colonial and "independent" Africa, to constitute, out of our "essential problems," the central and guiding questions of African philosophic thought.

In *our* specific political and historic context and beyond the rather sterile dispute between Ethnophilosophy and its scientistic critics, it is important to note that the concerns of contemporary African philosophy are focused on the possibility of overcoming the misery and political impotence of *our* present post-colonial situation. The veracity of this conviction is grounded on the fact that for Africa and Africans today the question against which life is staked is that of the political, economic, and cultural-existential survival of the continent. For ultimately, in the measured words of Antonio Gramsci:

> The philosophy of an historical epoch [i.e., in our case, post-colonial Africa] is . . . nothing other than the "history" of that epoch itself. . . . History and philosophy are in this sense indivisible: they form a bloc.[23]

Hence, in its impotent actuality, post-colonial Africa poses the challenge of self-transformation and the concrete actualization of its present chimerical "independence." On the level of thought this puts into question the inherited and taken for granted self-conception of African "liberation" as the guise and mask of neocolonialism. It does so, furthermore, in view of the suffering millions that have been victimized by the lived *actuality* as opposed to the hoped for *ideality* of an "independent" Africa.

It is in this painful gap between ideality and actuality that the hermeneutics of African philosophy finds its source and the locus of its concerns. This is also the gap it hopes to surmount on its own level of theoretic reflection. As Aimé Césaire has insightfully observed, "more and more the old négritude is turning into a corpse."[24] But the new "négritude" is yet to be born and in this historical interlude, African humanity is anxious and does not find itself at home. It is this felt anxiety, this absence, this gap between *actuality* and *ideality* which today calls forth and motivates the struggle, at various levels and in differing forms, against neocolonialism, and simultaneously, out of the exigencies of this struggle, provokes the reflections of African philosophical hermeneutics.

In terms of all that has been said thus far, the challenge of our post-colonial situation is grounded in the failed actuality of the promise of African independence. It is, in the words of Kwame Anthony Appiah, the manifestation of "a fundamental revolt against the endless misery of the last thirty years."[25] Thirty years ago, in the section of *The Wretched of the Earth* entitled "The Pitfalls of National Consciousness," Fanon had accurately anticipated the proper analysis for these decades of existential misery and political impotence. In like manner, out of the exigencies of the struggle against Portuguese colonialism, Cabral, twenty-six years ago, affirmed categorically that:

> We do not confuse exploitation or exploiters with the colour of men's skins; we do not want any exploitation in our countries, not even by black people.[26]

The remedy that both of these thinkers suggest—as appropriate then as now—out of the specificity of their respective contexts is that, in Fanon's words, we "turn over a new leaf" and "work out new concepts"[27] and in so doing invent the concrete actuality of our own existence. In thinking the historicity out of which it is being secreted, African philosophy is concretely engaged in doing precisely this— working out "new concepts."

In recognizing the situatedness of our own lived historicity as the proper object of reflection for African philosophic thought, we have actively inherited and made our own—within the context of the present—the as of yet unrealized grounding concerns of the discourse of the African liberation struggle. To this extent and specifically, the hermeneutics of contemporary African philosophy or African philosophical hermeneutics is a critical appropriation of the emancipatory possibilities of this discourse. Let me conclude this introduction, then, by very briefly outlining the thematic structure and expositional layout of this study as a whole.

III

Chapter 1 examines the grounding relation that philosophic thought has with the actuality out of which it is articulated. This question is explored in terms of the theoretic and lived reality out of which the reflections of African philosophic thought are produced.

Chapter 2, by way of further substantiating this point, explores the thematic connection of the discourse of the African liberation struggle to the contemporary discussions in African philosophy. The chapter presents a critical discussion and a critique of African philosophy which is focused on its thematic links to the failings and theoretic shortcomings of the discourse of the African liberation struggle.

Thus these first two chapters critically explore the mediated and mediating reflexive role of African philosophy in and out of the context of its own lived situatedness. In this regard they are an attestation to the lived hermeneuticity of the contemporary discourse of African philosophy.

Chapter 3 examines the dialectic of colonialist violence and the emancipatory counter-violence it evokes and the vital role played by this process in terminating not only the physical but the cultural-existential presence of the colonizer in the colonized. The central concern of this chapter is to show that violence has an indispensable and structuring function in both the process of casting the colonizer and the colonized and in the contrary effort aimed at molding the humanity of the human in the colonized and, no less, in the colonizer.

Chapter 4 examines the process by which the African liberation struggle, both against colonialism and neocolonialism, is a world-disclosing phenomenon that offers the possibility of concretely reclaiming and establishing the historicity of African existence in the contemporary world. It is an exploration of the concrete process by which the *Being* (i.e., the freedom) of African existence (i.e., its historicity) can be reclaimed and established anew out of the exigencies of the present.

Thus these last two chapters are hermeneutic elucidations of the possibility of African freedom that take their point of departure from positive aspects of the African liberation struggle. Specifically, these chapters are grounded on the seminal and hermeneutically insightful works of Frantz Fanon and Amilcar Cabral. The effort of these last two chapters is not merely to restate ideas, but to think further the concerns incarnated in these ideas by critically and eclectically pressing into service, for this purpose, insights derived and culled from the European philosophic tradition.

The reader should thus not be surprised to find, throughout this study, positive references and appropriations, as well as critical rejections of the European philosophic tradition. For ultimately, as Cornel West correctly points out, this obsessive (Afrocentric?) effort to bracket Europe at all costs is itself the product of our encounter with and interiority to Europe.[28] To be a Westernized African in today's post-colonial Africa means ultimately to be marked/branded—in one way or another—by the historical experience of European colonialism. We should not try to "hide" from this all pervasive element of our modern African historicity. Rather, our efforts to surmount it must begin by facing up to and confronting this enigmatic actuality. This then is the hermeneutic task of this study, for ultimately the antidote is always located in the poison!

In all of this, following Fanon and Cabral, I take my methodological cue from the "various attitudes that the Negro [African] adopts in contact with white civilization."[29] Thus, in sum, the phenomenality of African existence marked by colonialism and bludgeoned by neocolonialism is the central focus of my hermeneutical explorations. It is not, however, the lived psychopathology of these encounters but the emancipatory possibilities inscribed in them that is my main concern.

The conclusion will thus present, as its title suggests, the obverse of this introduction. It will briefly state, in view of the terrain of contemporary philosophy, the destructuring possibilities of African philosophic thought. For to effectively be a hermeneutic supplement to the enduring efforts against colonialism and neocolonialism is, simultaneously, to engage in the systematic enlargement and compounding of the fissures and contradictions interior to the Eurocentric and universalistic tradition of Western metaphysics.[30] After all, when all is said and done, this is the lived heritage which buttressed and gave ethical and metaphysical endorsement to the expansionist adventures of a colonialist Europe.

1

Philosophy and Post-colonial Africa Historicity and Thought

> For one thing, nothing could be done without friends and loyal companions, and such men were not easy to find ready at hand, since our city was no longer administered according to the standards and practices of our fathers.
>
> —Plato
> Letter VII, 325d

For us, contemporary Africans, the condition that has resulted from the colonial obliteration of the "standards and practices of our fathers," to use Plato's words, and the consequent neocolonial inertness of our contemporary situation is the necessary point of departure for any worthwhile or meaningful philosophic engagement. Thus, the closing years of the twentieth century are bound to be for Africa and Africans a time of prolonged, deep reflection and self-examination. Having achieved political "independence," for the most part, we now need to take stock of the victories, defeats, and compromises that constitute and inform our enigmatic present.

The concern with this felt and lived situation seems to be the central focus of post-colonial African literature and intellectual work as a whole. In fact, contemporary developments in African philosophy are themselves interior to this intellectual productivity and occupy a place of fundamental importance in it.[1] However, what has been said thus far notwithstanding, Marcien Towa has correctly observed that

> Africa will not really attain its cultural [historic, political, and economic] maturity as long as it does not elevate itself resolutely to

13

a profound thinking of its essential problems, that is to say, to philosophical reflection.[2]

In endorsing Towa's observation, we impose on ourselves the responsibility of properly articulating what these "essential problems" might be and of spelling out the role of "philosophical reflection" in the situation of the present. It was in the guise of introducing the "maturity" of the modern age that European colonialism imposed on Africa its present subordinate status. Thus, to be able to transcend this deplorable situation we contemporary Africans need to confront the question of our "maturity" at its most fundamental level—on the plane of philosophic reflection.

In this initial chapter, I will articulate the situated historicity of contemporary African philosophy as the critical self-reflection of a concrete totality: post-colonial Africa. In doing so, I will establish the parameters within which, in my view, Africa can "elevate itself resolutely to a profound thinking of its essential problems." It is only thus that it can self-consciously confront the question of its historic, cultural, political, and economic subordinate status or "maturity" imposed on it by colonialism, which to this day defines, in all spheres of life, the situation of the present.

I

As far back as 1958, Frantz Fanon had correctly pointed out, without the benefit of hindsight and from within the lived actuality of the African liberation struggle, that

> The twentieth century, when the future looks back on it, will not only be remembered as the era of atomic discoveries and interplanetary explorations. The second upheaval of this period, unquestionably, is the conquest by the peoples of the lands that belong to them.[3]

But the future will also note—as we do today in the last decade of the twentieth century—that the "conquest by the peoples of the lands that belong to them" was a much more complicated and protracted struggle than it first appeared to be.[4] When "the future looks back on it"— that is, on Fanon's present and our (1990s) immediate post-colonial past—it will register a rather harsh disillusionment and disappointment regarding the promise and the actuality of the immediate post-colonial African situation.[5] For as Enrique Dussel points out:

> The heroes of neocolonial emancipation worked in an ambiguous political sphere. Mahatma Gandhi in India, Abdel Nasser in Egypt, and Patrice Lumumba in the Congo dream of emancipation but are not aware that their nations will [soon] pass from the hands of England, France, or Belgium into the hands of the United States.[6]

Today, in the last decade of the twentieth century, the United States is the dominant superpower and the harbinger of a "new world order" dominated by the West (i.e., NATO).[7] In fact, paraphrasing Lenin and Nkrumah, one could describe this "new world order" as the latest, if not the highest, stage of neocolonialism in which the United States, under the guise of the United Nations, rules the world, and smart bombs enforce "international law." In this context,

> the prolongation of existing socio-economic structures and world relationships, deriving as these do from the colonial period and the world capitalist structure, must inevitably, without a change, produce in Africa a vast international slum.[8]

In fact, the 1970s and the 1980s have already been for Africa a period of "endemic famine"[9] orchestrated by the criminal incompetence and political subservience of African governments—to European, North American, and Soviet interests. Thus, irony of ironies, the official inheritors of the legacy of the African liberation struggle today preside over—or, more appropriately, dictate—the neocolonial demise of the continent. This is the paradox and "dark" enigma of contemporary Africa.

It is appropriate then for the closing decade of the twentieth century to be a period of introspection and self-examination. For the naive mid-century euphoria of "liberation" and "freedom" has come to naught. It has been callously dashed on the historically languid violence of neocolonialism. These very terms, "liberation" and "freedom"— the proud, clear, and popular slogans of yesterday's anti-colonial struggle—are today's opaque, obscure, and ambiguous enigma. In the midst of famine, political terror, Western or Eastern ("democratic" or "socialist," as the case may be) military interventions, "liberation" and "freedom" have become the words with which Occidental power imperiously proclaims its military might and political preeminence.

In contrast to the recent past (i.e., the period of armed anti-colonial liberation struggles), today it is in these very terms that post-colonial "independent" Africa misunderstands itself. What seemed to be clear and unambiguous has become obscure and opaque. Thus the lethargic inertness of neocolonialism passes for the actuality of "freedom" and "liberation." To explore and decipher the source of this vexing "misunderstanding" is the proper task of contemporary African philosophy. For it is only by challenging and contesting this situation at its source that Africa can put behind it the subordinate status imposed on it by European colonialism and perpetuated by neocolonialism.

As Hans-Georg Gadamer, the father of contemporary philosophical hermeneutics puts it, it is precisely this negative situation of "misunderstanding" and the estrangement of meaning within the lived context of a tradition (i.e., a specific historicalness) which is the originative moment of hermeneutics as a particular philosophic orientation. For Gadamer, "understanding becomes a special task only when . . . misunderstandings have arisen."[10] What Gadamer is here enunciating is the grounding insight of the tradition of philosophical hermeneutics within which he operates.[11] This insight is an old, even if at times neglected, truth of philosophy that is abundantly epitomized in the originative moments of Plato's dialogues (which occupy a central paradigmatic place in Gadamer's work) and is categorically affirmed by Hegel when he writes that: "Diremption is the source of *the need for philosophy.*"[12]

In our case, the veracity of the above is confirmed by the indisputable historical and violent diremption effected by colonialism and the continued "misunderstanding" of our situation perpetuated by neocolonialism which calls forth and provokes thought in post-colonial Africa.[13] It is in this regard, then, that the proper task of philosophy in Africa is that of systematically elaborating a radical hermeneutics of the contemporary African situation. Having asserted the central and defining claim of this study, we now have to confront Gadamer's strong reservations on this point and the rather contentious remarks of the African historian and philosopher Ernest Wamba-Dia-Wamba.

II

Gadamer forcefully affirms that "hermeneutics has [now] become fashionable and every interpretation [today, 1977] wants to call itself 'hermeneutical.' "[14] On the other hand, Wamba rhetorically asks, almost a decade later, in 1983: Why is hermeneutics "understood by our African philosophers" as the correct response "to the philosophical question in Africa?"[15] From these remarks, especially from Wamba's observations, we can surmise that a hermeneutical orientation, for better or for worse, has already taken root within the indigenous soil of the discourse of contemporary African philosophy.[16]

The net rhetorical effect of these strong remarks, however (expressed, as they are, from within differing philosophical paradigms: philosophical hermeneutics and an "Africanized" Marxism-Leninism), is to question the validity of the "linkage" of hermeneutics to African philosophy. Gadamer charges that hermeneutics is now in vogue and points to a faddish fashionableness without substance. Wamba, on the other hand, following his rhetorical question and without in any way philosophically accounting for the ideological bent of his own ties to European thought, strongly suggests that a hermeneutical position in African philosophy lacks "authenticity" and does not escape neocolonialism: European tutelage in the realm of theory.

The validity—both philosophic and political—of the "link" between hermeneutics and African philosophy is thus in doubt. Given the nature of my concerns—named by the title: *The Hermeneutics of African Philosophy: Horizon and Discourse*—it is necessary and beneficial in this initial chapter, to begin by presenting a sustained defense against this double, if disparate, attack. In so doing I will formulate the question of hermeneutics (my response to Gadamer) and of the hermeneuticity of contemporary African philosophy (my response to Wamba) by concretely exploring the way in which philosophic discourse itself originates from and is organically linked to the concrete conditions-of-existence and the life-practices of the horizon within and out of which it is formulated. I will also show, in the process of articulating the above and in line with my subtitle, that this hermeneutical undertaking cannot but be a politically committed and historically specific critical self-reflection that stems from the negativity of our post-colonial present.

III

The hermeneuticity of contemporary African philosophy—as is the case with the hermeneuticity of philosophical discourse as such—consists of the interplay of horizon and discourse. This interplay is grounded on the concrete and lived historicalness of a specific horizon. The terms "horizon" and "discourse," are here used in a rather specialized sense. Horizon designates the historico-hermeneutical and politi-co-cultural milieu within and out of which specific discourses (philo-sophic, artistic, scientific, etc.) are articulated. It is the overall existential space within and out of which they occur. Discourse, on the other hand, refers to these articulated concerns interior to the concrete conditions-of-existence made possible by and internal to a specific horizon.[17]

The discourse of modern European philosophy, beginning with Des-cartes, for example, originates in the concerns arising from the horizon of modern science. Out of these concerns, associated with the names of Galileo and Newton, the discourse of modern philosophy is articu-lated.[18] It is these concerns that provoked and made possible Kant's Copernican Revolution in philosophy and enshrined the subjectivity of the subject as the originative moment of reflection for modern European thought.

In like manner, but within a radically different horizon, the philo-sophic discourses of the sixteenth-century Abyssinian philosopher Zar'a Ya'aqob and his disciple Walda Heywat are grounded in the lived concerns of their day. Unlike their European counterparts, the Abyssinian thinkers are concerned with questions of piety and the nature of faith in the context of the acute crisis of Abyssinian Christian-ity, in confrontation with the subversive work of Jesuit missionaries and aggressive Catholicism. Religiosity, in its differing and thus bewil-dering claims, manifestations, and contradictory instantiations, is the singular and defining concern of Zar'a Ya'aqob's and Walda Heywat's thinking.[19]

In our case, on the other hand, it is neither the theoretical exigencies of modern science, nor the crisis of faith in confrontation with a foreign and aggressive piety that provokes thought. Rather, it is the politico-existential crisis interior to the horizon of post-colonial Africa which brings forth the concerns and originates the theoretic space for the discourse of contemporary African philosophy. In each case then, it is out of the concerns and needs of a specific horizon that a particular philosophic discourse is articulated. For as Elungu Pene Elungu puts it:

> It is often during periods of perturbation that the human being is called on to affirm and at the same time verify the unfathomable depth from whence springs his action on the world, on himself and on others.[20]

In a similar way Theophilus Okere points out that the various dis-courses of philosophy are "dictated by the non-philosophy [i.e., horizon]" which is "their own cultural [and historical] background."[21] Elungu and Okere articulate, in slightly differing formulations, the same insight: philosophic discourse is a reflexive and reflective response to the felt crisis of a lived and concrete horizon.

In view of the above then, to interpretatively engage the present situation in terms of what Africa "*has been*"[22]—both in its ambiguous pre-colonial "greatness"[23] as well as in its colonial and neocolonial demise—is the proper hermeneutical task of African philosophical thought. This interpretative exploration, furthermore, has to be undertaken in view of the future of freedom toward which Africa aspires— as exemplified by its undaunted struggle, and in spite of all its failings, against colonialism and neocolonialism. This historically saturated, explorative self-reflection is the basic character of philosophy, whether consciously recognized as such or not, and constitutes the explicit self-awareness of hermeneutics as a philosophic orientation.[24]

This then is the radical hermeneutic task of contemporary African philosophy in view of the contradictory and yet fecund legacy of the African liberation struggle. Radical, because such a task is concerned with exploring and exposing the root-sources of the contradictions of our paradoxical present. Hermeneutical, because such a grounding exploration cannot but be a constant and ongoing interpretative and reinterpretative task undertaken in view of the failures and successes of our history as Africans in the contemporary world. As Okonda Okolo puts it:

> The cultural [historic] memory is ceaselessly renewed retroactively by new discoveries. Our past, by continually modifying itself through our discoveries, invites us to new appropriations; these appropriations lead us toward a better grasp of our identity.[25]

In this respect, then, the hermeneutical task of contemporary African philosophy is itself interior to the lived and continuous process of self-understanding indigenous to a particular historicalness, to a specific identity.

It is this perpetual process of lived self-understanding, peculiar and internal to human existence as such, that philosophical hermeneutics consciously articulates and cultivates. Moreover, this is the concrete actuality of the contemporary discourse of African philosophy insofar as it is concerned with overcoming the diremptions and misunderstandings of present-day Africa—what Wiredu and Hountondji respectively refer to as the "anachronism" of our situation and the "folklorism"[26] of our theoretic efforts.

The fundamental orientation of this inherently interpretative under-taking is aimed at disclosing a future in congruence with the humanity of the human in African existence. But one might and indeed should ask at this point: What exactly does humanity mean in this context? In this regard I take my cue not from Leopold Sedar Senghor's essentialist humanism of "negroness" (*Négritude*), but from Martin Heidegger's ontological and phenomenological formulation (itself the product of a systematic hermeneutic of modern European existence), that "*the substance of man [the human being] is existence,*"[27] or, put differently, "The 'essence' [*Wesen*] of this entity lies in its 'to be' [*Zu-sein*]."[28] Heidegger's personal political languidity and Eurocentric anti-semitic racist views notwithstanding,[29] his formulation of the Being (*Sein*) of the human being is grounded in the particular ontological specificity of the temporalizing ecstatic phenomenality of human existence.[30] To the extent that we recognize both Europe and Africa as sites of human historical becoming, the ontological explorations of the "to be" of human existence, which Heidegger undertakes from within the ontic confines of European modernity, can also be posed from within the ontic confines of other cultures and histories.[31]

In his destructuring reading of the tradition of European metaphys-ics, starting from the lived ecstatic phenomenality of human life, Hei-degger asserts—against the ossified and ossifying ontotheological con-ceptions of human existence—that human reality (*Dasein*) is not a present-at-hand substance or entity, but the lived fluidity/actuality of its own existence. In this radical destructive hermeneutic critique of the metaphysical tradition, Heidegger explores—in *Being and Time* and in his later works—the "to be" [*Zu-sein*] of European modernity. Seen from the perspective of Heidegger's Being-question, and the grounding ontic-ontological destructive analysis that derives from it, the modern world is caught in the snare of the *Ge-stell* (en-framing) of modern technology. Thus, the evocations of Heidegger's Being-question are aimed at salvaging the "to be" (i.e., the essential nonsub-stantial substance) of European modernity from the beguiling snare of technological catastrophe. To the very end, Heidegger's efforts were dominated by and directed against this obstinate *Ge-stell*, and oriented toward the striving "to prepare the possibility of a transformed abode of man in the world."[32]

We too—the ex-colonial subjects of this ensnared and ensnaring Europe—suffer from this *Ge-stell*. But for us this situation of en-framing is mediated, instituted, and imposed through the persistence of neocolonialism as the continued intrusion of European hegemony in present-day Africa. This hegemony—beyond the overt violence of colonialism and in a much more effective manner—institutes and establishes itself from within and reproduces and perpetuates our subordinate status in the contemporary world. Thus, for us to appropriate the "to be" of our historicalness means to confront European neocolonial subjugation: the politics of economic, cultural, and scientific subordination.

The insidious nature of neocolonialism is that it internally replicates—in an indigenous guise—what previously was imposed from the outside by the exclusive and explicit use of violence. In view of the above then, and unlike Heidegger, for us, the question of our existence, of our "to be," is an inherently political question. To neglect the politics of this question, in our case, is to disregard the question itself. For, when we ask or reflect on our own humanity, when we examine the actuality, the "substance of our existence" as human beings, there we find and are confronted by an internalized imperious Europe dominant over the contradictory remains of our own indigent and subjected indigenousness.

It is in this manner that the *Ge-stell* of modern technology shows itself, and is rendered in the form of political domination. As Wamba puts it:

> This is why the expatriate personnel, from imperialist countries, are more at ease in these national [African] state structures, functioning as if they were made by, and for, that personnel, than are the majority of the natives who have to bear [and support] these structures' repressive hierarchical weight. In these conditions, to be intelligent, reasonable, rational, civilized, etc., is to be receptive to, and to function according to, the logic and rationality governing these [neocolonial] structures.[33]

This tragicomic obscene duplication of Europe—in Africa and as Africa—is the actual and concrete duplicity which negatively constitutes and positively structures the nonhistoricity of neocolonialism—its historico-existential inertness.

In this manner the technocratic *Ge-stell* of European modernity—compounded by and in the form of political, economic, cultural, and historical dominance—is imposed on us, the ex-colonial subjects of imperial Europe. In the name and in the guise of technological and scientific "assistance" Europe imposes on us its hegemonic political and cultural control. We are thus afflicted by proxy. Precisely for this reason, a concrete hermeneutics of the existentiality of our existence, in order to be adequate, has to confront the actuality of our present. For the "veracity" of this present is the historical duplicity of neocolonialism, which is lived and concretely actualized in and through our existence.[34] In this context the culture of the former colonial power is the ground and the accepted source of hegemonic cultural, technical-economic, and historico-political dominance.

This is the historical and cultural estrangement, internal to our situation, that Fanon systematically inspected as early as 1952 in *Black Skin, White Masks*. It is the estranged and estranging tragic legacy of the European "civilizing mission" to the world. As Basil Davidson points out, the African anti-colonial struggle did not only expel the physical presence of colonialism, but it also put in

> question the smoothly borrowed assumptions of the social hybrids [i.e., Europeanized Africans] about the opposition of "European civilization" to "African barbarism."[35]

Indeed, beyond the physical combat to expel colonialism, contemporary Africa finds itself confronted and hindered, at every turn, by that which this combat has put in question without fundamentally and decisively eradicating.

Thus, present-day African realities are constituted partly by the hybrid remnants of the colonial and pre-colonial past—as embodied at every level in the ossified neocolonial institutional forms of contemporary Africa and in the pathologically negative self-awareness of Europeanized Africans—and partly by the varied forms of struggle aimed at actualizing the possibility of an autonomous and free Africa in the context of the contemporary world. These struggles, furthermore, are not homogenous in their ideological or theoretic orientation. Along with the Africanist essentialism of Senghor, we have Nkrumah's Marxism-Leninism, as well as the historically and hermeneutically astute theoretic perspectives articulated by Fanon and Cabral. All this and more is the mélange that constitutes the lived actuality of post-colonial Africa!

Broadly speaking then, this is the enigmatic and paradoxical inheritance of African "independence": the situation of the present. It is the "ambiguous adventure" of Africa that Cheikh Hamidou Kane articulates so well in his seminal novel of the same title. The inseminative tilling of Africa's "ambiguous adventure" with the Occident is thus the central concern of contemporary African philosophy. It is only by hermeneutically plowing (i.e., turning over) and radically subverting the theoretic space of the post-colonial African situation, with the concrete historicity of our own most distinctive existential actuality that African philosophic reflection can be part of the practical and theoretic effort aimed at concretely reclaiming the freedom and actuality of the continent.

In the words of Antonio Gramsci:

> The beginning of a critical elaboration is the awareness of that which really is, that is to say a "knowing of one's self" as a product of the process of history that has unfolded thus far and which has left in you an infinity of traces collected without the benefit of an inventory. It is necessary initially to undertake such an inventory.

> Note II. One cannot separate philosophy from the history of philosophy and culture from the history of culture. In a more direct and fitting or proper sense, it is not possible to be philosophers, that is, to have a critically coherent conception of the world, without a consciousness of its historicity, of the phase of development represented by it and of the fact that it is in contradiction with other conceptions or with elements of other conceptions.[36]

In this regard, African philosophy can be true to its own historicity—the historicalness of contemporary Africa out of which it is being secreted and spun—by concretely exploring and confronting the "infinity of traces" left by colonialism and the enduring remains of the pre-colonial past. It is, in this manner, a "knowing of one's self" and an explorative "inventory" aimed at appropriating that which is possible in the context of a specific history.

As Gramsci puts it, "philosophy is the critique and the surpassing [*superamento,* i.e., the Hegelian notion of sublation] of religion and of common sense and in this way it coincides with 'good sense' [*buon senso*] which is counterpoised to common sense."[37] This is so, inasmuch as the "religion" of the mass and a historically specific "common sense" are the culturally distinctive self-awareness of a people that structures its historic and politico-economic existence internal to its traditions. Philosophy is thus this critical and explorative engagement of one's own cultural specificity and lived historicalness. It is a critically aware explorative appropriation of our cultural, political, and historical existence.

In view of the above, contemporary African philosophy has to be conceived as a radically originative hermeneutics of the paradoxical and yet fecund post-colonial present. It is the ardent effort to reclaim the African experience of Being—the historicity of the various modes of African existence—from within the world-historical context of the present, i.e., the implosion of European modernity. In other words, it is an attempt to explore and concretely reappropriate what this modernity closed off at the dawn of its own originative moment of history: the violent self-inception of its own historical actualization.[38]

In this regard, the hermeneutics of contemporary African philosophy or African philosophical hermeneutics is a thinking of new beginnings born out of our enigmatic political "emancipation" and the historical and political crisis of European modernity—the long-awaited weakening, if not the demise, of our subjugators. As Okolo sagaciously points out:

> In Africa, the interest in hermeneutics also arises out of the reality of crisis: a generalized identity crisis due to the presence of a culture— a foreign and dominating tradition—and the necessity for a self-affirmation in the construction of an authentic culture and tradition.[39]

In the paragraph that precedes the sentence just quoted, Okolo points out that in Europe, the "birth and current revival of the hermeneutic movement" is linked to crises: "the crisis of self-identity in German romanticism," and the "crisis of Europe confronted with a technicized [technicises] world and language," which Heidegger, among others, "felt . . . as the forgetting of Being."[40] In each case then, and in terms of differing traditions, the hermeneuticity of philosophy is grounded on the theoretic effort to reconstruct and appropriate meaning within the parameters of a lived inheritance and tradition that has become estranged and crisis prone. In other words, philosophic discourse does not just happen; rather, it is the articulation of reflective concerns interior to a negativity arising out of the horizon of a specific cultural and historical totality within which it is located and framed.[41]

For philosophic reflection, the lived life concerns of a culture, a history, a tradition, serve as the source and bedrock on which its own hermeneuticity is grounded. Thus, philosophic discourse is the rhetorically effective enunciation—the bringing to utterance—of the historicity of existence out of and within a specific historicalness. For as Okolo emphatically affirms, ultimately, "hermeneutics [philosophy] exists only in particular traditions."[42]

In view of the fact that one dwells and is immured within the bounds and lived confines of one's tradition or concrete historicalness, how precisely does the hermeneutically oriented philosopher engage the particular tradition or historicalness within which and out of which philosophizing occurs? In this regard, in *An Introduction to Metaphysics,* Heidegger writes:

> But here we may, indeed, we must ask: Which interpretation is the true one, the one which simply takes over a perspective into which it has fallen, because this perspective, this line of sight, presents itself as familiar and self-evident; or the interpretation which questions the customary perspective from top to bottom, because conceivably— and indeed actually—this line of sight does not lead to what is in need of being seen.[43]

In other words, the philosopher/interpreter who works out of the context of the present, as it relates to and arises out of a specific tradition, should not passively adhere to what is given by that tradition. Rather, the relation to tradition is an open-ended encounter in which what is explicitly preserved and implicitly betrayed by tradition is revealed. But how or from what vantage point is the "customary perspective" to be questioned from "top to bottom"?

> This is not done shiftily and arbitrarily, nor is it done by clinging to a system set up as a norm, but in and out of historical necessity (*Notwendigkeit*), out of the need (*Not*) of historical being-there.[44]

It is imperative for us to note that by "historical being-there," Heidegger means the concrete and factual (ontic) situation in which human beings find themselves (i.e., the actual lived situation of an individual or a group) within the confines and possibilities of a specific tradition.

In other words, "historical being-there" (i.e., a specific person or a historical community of persons) always becomes what it is by projecting itself out of its effective past, its lived inheritance. Its "destiny" is thus always what comes out of itself, its "has been," out of the prospects of its history and the possibilities of its generation. As Okolo explains, "destiny" is here understood as the

> implacable given [actuality] of a people and of an individual, but it is also a task of the future for a people and for an individual. It is the thread of tradition and of interpretations.[45]

It is in a constant process of self-interpretation and ongoing re-interpretations that a history, a people (and an individual within the confines of a people and a generation), constitutes itself and projects its future/destiny—the yet-to-be of its lived presence.

Taking Heidegger's *Being and Time* as his benchmark, Gadamer refers to the actuality of "historical being-there," in its encounter with tradition, as the "effective-historical consciousness."[46] For Gadamer the "effective-historical consciousness" or the hermeneutical encounter with tradition is open to the tradition's claim to truth. In this encounter, tradition/history (i.e., the written or oral past) is not muffled but allowed to challenge the certainties of the present. The interpreter or philosopher in this situation—the embodiment of the "effective-historical consciousness"—is in a questioning and yet released disposition to that which the past holds in its independence and the autonomy of its possibilities.

This openness and willingness to *risk* the standpoint of the present is the critical moment and the moment of critique in the hermeneutical encounter with tradition. The undecided and risky character of the hermeneutical situation, furthermore, arises out of the concrete "need [*Not*]" of the actuality of estrangement, out of which tradition, as the historicalness of the present, is explored and engaged.[47] As I have already pointed out, for us contemporary Africans, that which impels us to thought is precisely the estranged actuality of our present deriving from the colonial experience, the specific particularity of our history. Thus, it is in view of the inert presence of neocolonialism—the diremptions and misunderstandings consequent on colonialism—that a radical hermeneutics becomes the proper task of contemporary African philosophy.

It is necessary at this point to confront squarely the fundamental problem of this whole explication: How can one guard against the political dangers latent in an open-ended and radically interpretative relation with a particular and specific tradition exclusively guided by the "need [*Not*]" of the contemporary moment of history? Or as Drew Hyland puts it, how is "the 'ontic' [concrete, political, and historical] question of good and evil" to be settled?[48]

One can only say that it is the "effective-history,"[49] to use Gadamer's term, the history that makes itself felt and saturates the lived presence and actuality of the present (in our case, the emancipatory promise and failure of the African liberation struggle) that acts as the normative standard which projects a future/destiny as the actuality of its yet-to-be. This effective past, this felt presence of history, itself is derived from and simultaneously constitutes our hermeneutical appropriation of the heritage that we project as our future.

In other words, if "historical being-there" (i.e., the concretely situated person in community) projects itself out of its past (i.e., out of that which marks the present by its presence while being appropriated by it as its concretely felt "effective-history"), it follows that the emancipatory aspirations of this effective past have a defining and normatively determining relation to our future, our destiny. As Okolo unequivocally points out, our

> hermeneutical situation is that of the formerly colonized, the oppressed, that of the underdeveloped, struggling for more justice and equality. From this point of view, the validity of an interpretation is tied to the validity of a struggle—of its justice and of its justness. Here, we affirm the methodological preeminence of praxis on hermeneutics, praxis understood in the sense of an action tending toward the qualitative transformation of life.[50]

In this context, as Okolo affirms, "Hermeneutical theory is an integral part of hermeneutical practice. Here, theory is not added to practice as a luxurious supplement; it illuminates practice, which, in turn provokes it in a dialectical manner."[51] In this theoretic scenario, emancipatory *praxis* opens and offers the timely issues and concerns in which a hermeneutical perspective incarnates its interrogative and interpretative explorations. Conversely, and as a rejoinder to the dialectical tensions interior to this relation, hermeneutical reflection opens to *praxis* the proper theoretic space to explore and suggest the normative alignment of its emancipatory projects and practical undertakings.

It is imperative to remember, as Amilcar Cabral unequivocally pointed out in 1962, that the *praxis* of the African anti-colonial struggle as affirmed by the "UN resolution on decolonialisation" is now part of the internationally recognized emancipatory legacy of post-colonial humanity.[52] In honoring this legacy we are basically upholding the "justice" and "justness" of our age-old African struggle against colonialism and the continuing efforts against neocolonialism. In view of this:

> When in our country [or Continent] a comrade dies under police torture, is assassinated in prison, is burned alive or falls under the bullets of Portuguese guns, for which cause is he giving his life? He is giving it for the liberation of our people from the colonial yoke, and hence for the UN. In fighting and dying for the liberation of

> our countries we are giving our lives, in the present context of
> international legality, for the ideal which the UN itself has defined
> in its Charter, in its resolutions, and in particular in its resolution
> on decolonialisation.[53]

The struggle against neocolonialism is, furthermore, a continuation
and a hermeneutically critical refining of this emancipatory *praxis*
aimed at autonomy and freedom in full recognition of the differing
cultural-historical totalities that constitute our world. This then is the
moment of critique in the hermeneutical encounter with tradition and
the specifics of appropriation within a particular historicalness.

In contradistinction to Heidegger then, and with Cabral and Fanon,
on an *ontic* level it is our struggle, grounded in the specificity of
our history, which acts as the normative sieve that strains, sifts, and
negotiates our orientation to the future. This does not mean that we
cling "to a system set up as a norm,"[54] nor that we are beguiled by
history, wheresoever it might take us! Rather, in releasing ourselves
to the fluidity of our existence and of our future, in and out of this
fluidity we firmly resolve that the lived "necessity [*Notwendigkeit*]"[55]
out of which this future is being historicized will always be remem-
bered. In so doing we persevere and sustain into the future the "justice"
and the "justness" of our concrete engagements. This is how we re-
spond to Hyland's germane question regarding "good and evil."[56]

Thus, African philosophy as the hermeneutics of the post-colonial
situation is the critical remembrance, itself interior to the lived emancipatory *praxis* of contemporary Africa, that cultivates, mediates, and
revitalizes the origin or the source of this emancipatory *praxis* as the
historicity of its effective inheritance. It is the discourse which concretely evokes and evocatively recalls to this emancipatory tradition
the "truth" of its originative disclosure. Occasioned by the felt and lived
needs of the present, it explores the future embedded and preserved in
the possibilities of the heritage of its own enduring horizon. In so doing
it explodes the duplicity and sterility of the neocolonial duplication of
European modernity (i.e., the en-framing of modern technology) and
inaugurates "invention into [contemporary African] existence."[57]

As we shall see in chapter 4, this is how the African liberation
struggle—as critically epitomized in the thinking of Fanon and Cabral—actualizes the historicity of the colonized in the process of the
anti-colonial struggle. In the apt words of Cheikh Hamidou Kane:
"*We* have not had the same past, *you* and ourselves, but we shall have,
strictly, the same future. The era of separate destinies has run its course

. . . no one can any longer live by the simple carrying out of what he himself is." In the sameness of this global future, however, we the formerly colonized, "all of us, Hindus, Chinese, South Americans, Negroes, Arabs, all of us, awkward and pitiful, we the under-developed, who feel ourselves to be clumsy in a world of perfect mechanical adjustments," have to reclaim and concretely reinstitute the historicity of our own existence.[58]

This is the "justice" and "justness" that originates out of the disappointed possibilities of our past, from whence we project a future. A future in which the unequivocal recognition of the multiverse that constitutes our—thus far denied—historical and cultural specificity (i.e., our humanity) will become the basis for global earthly solidarity. Thus, heeding Fanon's insightful words, we leave behind Old Europe, with all its transcendental and empty odes to "Man,"[59] and with Nietzsche we *"remain faithful to the earth."*[60]

IV

The hermeneutical orientation in contemporary African philosophy or African philosophical hermeneutics is thus thematically and historically linked to the demise of direct European colonial dominance and is aimed at the destructuring of the persistence of neocolonial hegemony in contemporary African existence. It is focused on the theoretic consummation of this demise. For the concrete resurrection of Africa beyond the tutelage of Europe requires in all spheres of life a rethinking of the present asphyxiating inertness in terms which are conducive and congenial to Africa and its diverse peoples. This is the indispensable hermeneutic supplement to the historic and concrete process of "re-Africanisation"[61] without which, as Cabral tells us, nothing can be achieved.

As part of the cultural and intellectual production of a diverse continent, the hermeneutic evocations of the African philosopher are interior to the efforts of differing African peoples in "the sphere of thought" to constitute and "keep [themselves] . . . in existence."[62] For the African philosopher the accent is on hermeneutically exploring these differences in view of the common and binding African experience in confronting European modernity—the shared experience of colonialism and neocolonialism.

In the commonality of these differences we need to ascend to and forge a joint future. For beyond the inert present the future still remains "to be discovered."[63] As Okolo fittingly observes:

> We have to acknowledge that our efforts at theorizing interpretation and tradition are inscribed interior to the ways and means that tradition itself secretes and utilizes for its own preservation, renewal, and perpetuation.[64]

The basic task of philosophy in Africa is explicitly giving voice to this needful concern. In contributing to this hermeneutical effort, on its own level of abstraction and in full recognition of its lived historicity, philosophy constitutes itself and fulfills its calling—to think that which evokes thought—in the situatedness of the present. To affirm the above is to recognize that "interpretation [philosophy] presupposes a tradition, and . . . tradition as such is always interpreted."[65] This is the historicity of philosophic thought and reflection in the context of post-colonial Africa. For the historicity of philosophy is always measured against its own conscious awareness—or lack thereof—of its lived presuppositions and its rootedness in a specific tradition and history.

In view of all that has been said thus far, then, the discourse of African philosophy has to be grasped explicitly as a radical hermeneutics of the contemporary African situation. This historically specific situation is that out of which African philosophical hermeneutics spins the thread of its reflexive reflections. Taking its point of departure from the as of yet unfulfilled promise of African "independence," this hermeneutical perspective constitutes the substance of its discourse and critically appropriates as its own the emancipatory horizon of the theoretical and political legacy of the African liberation struggle.[66] As Heidegger aptly puts it:

> Philosophy will never seek to deny its "presuppositions," but neither may it simply admit them. It conceives them, and it unfolds with more and more penetration both the presuppositions themselves and that for which they are presuppositions.[67]

Thus far I have only arranged the overall structure of the "presuppositions" that underpin the hermeneutic perspective of this study. In what follows I will explore further and substantiate the position of African philosophical hermeneutics preliminarily articulated thus far.

2

African Philosophy
Horizon and Discourse

Then there is the case of the conquest and brutal destruction of economic resources, by which, in certain circumstances, a whole local or national economic development
could formerly be ruined. Nowadays [the late nineteenth
century] such a case usually has the opposite effect, at
least among great [European] peoples: in the long run
the vanquished [the Asiatic, the African . . . etc.] often
gains more economically, politically and morally than the
victor.

—Friedrich Engels
From a letter to Joseph Bloch, 1890

When the white serpent has once bitten you, you will
search in vain for a remedy against its bite.

—Bahta Hagos
Eritrean anti-colonialist leader, 1894

The period of world history that begins with the end of the Second
World War has been for Africa not a period of relative peace and
calm, but rather a period of accelerated war and political turmoil.[1]
To be sure, these conflicts have not been futile. By the end of the
1960s most of Africa had achieved the status of political independence and the early 1970s witnessed the end of Portugese-NATO
colonialism—the oldest European colonial empire in Africa.[2] The independence of Namibia in March 1990, the military-political victory
of the Eritrean resistance in May 1991, and the independence referen-
dum held in April 1993, along with the dynamic developments in

31

South Africa, all point to the possibility that the 1990s will be the decade in which not only European colonialism but differing forms of African colonialism and external domination will be totally eradicated.[3]

To this day, however, armed political conflicts—in the midst of famine and "natural" calamities—rage on.[4] Grim as this picture may be, it is important to remember that it constitutes the African peoples' varied and differing struggles to define and establish their freedom.[5] But what are the people of Africa trying to free themselves from and what are they trying to establish?

This "prior question," to use Plato's formulation, is squarely situated in the domain of philosophy and is the central question in the problematic of African freedom which will concern us in this chapter and in this study as a whole.[6] All those whose names, at various levels, have been associated with the African liberation struggle have had to seriously engage this question. Nkrumah, Senghor, Lumumba, Nyerere, Césaire, Fanon, Cabral, and the literature—which for us constitutes the theoretic legacy—of the African liberation struggle as a whole (i.e., pamphlets, programs, documents, manifestos, novels, poems, etc.), can all be read as a sustained effort to pose and politically confront this grounding question. In this question our aim is to confront Africa in "metamorphosis."[7]

This is necessary precisely because, without explicitly engaging the central concerns articulated by the theoretic and political legacy of the African liberation struggle, the contemporary debate in and on African philosophy ploughs this same terrain. In undertaking such a critical exploration we will locate the thematic ground of contemporary African philosophic debate in the theoretic cul-de-sac of the African liberation struggle. We will thus supplement the discussion of contemporary African philosophy presented in the introduction with its parallel ideological and political correlate. In order to attain some measure of succinctness if not completeness, my exposition will be centered on Kwame Nkrumah's Marxism-Leninism and Leopold Sedar Senghor's *Africanité* (or *Négritude*) and African Socialism.[8] These are the two politically contrary positions that encompass the legacy of the African liberation struggle as a whole.

The exposition will show that the theoretic positions of Nkrumah and Senghor have a parallel and intrinsic affinity to the "opposed" philosophic perspectives of Ethnophilosophy and Professional Philosophy. As we shall see, these parallel positions share, in contrary ways, a dilapidating Eurocentric metaphysics. This theoretic blind spot can be overcome only by grasping the historicalness of the African situation and orienting one's thinking accordingly. As already indicated in the introduction and in chapter 1, this is the theoretic project of African philosophical hermeneutics in the context of the contemporary debate in African philosophy.

I

In responding to the above-indicated foundational "prior question"—What are the people of Africa trying to free themselves from and what are they trying to establish?—as far back as 1945 in *Towards Colonial Freedom,* Kwame Nkrumah, a leading pioneer of the African anti-colonial struggle, had posed and formulated this question in strictly economic terms, out of an anti-imperialist orientation of Marxist-Leninist inspiration.[9] Twenty-five years later, in *Class Struggle in Africa* (1970), Nkrumah addressed this question in much the same way, but this time around in strictly Marxist-Leninist terms:

> In almost every African state, nonindependent and independent guerilla struggle is being prepared or has been established as the only means to overthrow colonialist, neocolonialist or settler regimes. . . . Guerilla activities will also continue in many of the independent states, so long as there is no attempt being made to have the means of production owned by the masses of the African people. Unless the leaders of the independent African states stop paying lip service to socialism and go all out for scientific socialism they are only deferring the guerilla onset.[10]

In making the above observation, Nkrumah was stating what indeed was the case on the continent as a whole: at the time he wrote, there were seventeen major liberation movements active in both independent and nonindependent Africa.[11]

Then as now, however, the language Nkrumah utilized fails to grapple with the historicity of the African situation. By unreservedly employing the abstract and worn out language of Marxism-Leninism, the language of "scientific socialism" and "means of production," and by framing the problematic of African freedom in these terms, Nkrumah occludes the foundational and grounding character of the question of freedom in Africa.

Nkrumah calls for "scientific socialism" precisely because he thinks it will empower the disinherited peoples of Africa to establish the possibility of their freedom, which he understands to be the control of the "means of production" by the "masses of the African people." However, in posing and framing the question in this manner and in the very act of formulating the question in this way, Nkrumah underinterprets the problematic of African freedom, and in so doing, banishes it to being nothing more than a "European" economic question in the tropics. In other words, Nkrumah implicitly universalizes and surreptitiously—without even the semblance of an argument— assumes the historic ground of European modernity: that the ground of "scientific socialism" is the universal ground on which and out of which economic questions *as such* are posed. Thus, the specific particularity of the African situation is relegated to oblivion.

Nkrumah's formulation is basically aimed at superimposing a general and abstract—universal, context-neutral, and value-free—theory on a specific and particular historico-cultural situation. Thus, the Eurocentric framework within which Nkrumah poses the problematic as a whole remains unquestioned, and yet it is silently and surreptitiously presupposed. In fact, it is that which grounds and slyly determines everything!

Nkrumah fails to ask what socialism or any other universal, neutral, and culture- and value-free conception of freedom conceived and constructed outside the concrete context of African historical existence could mean in and for the African situation. Along with most Marxist-Leninists, he fails to realize that a theory (any theory) always carries, sustains, valorizes, and constantly resuscitates within itself the traces of the originative historic ground out of which it was initially theorized. In the case of "scientific socialism," this is the historic ground of the Enlightenment—the ground of European modernity which then becomes the archetype of all "illumination" and freedom as such. In other words, "scientific socialism" automatically and of necessity privileges its own originative historic ground as metaphysically paradigmatic for human existence in all of its derivative applications.[12] Thus, to talk of "scientific socialism" in a singular and undifferentiated way—as Nkrumah does—is to superimpose European ideas and conceptions (in the guise of "objective" theory) on the African situation. In other words, the historical and cultural specificity of Africa and of the struggle for African freedom is obliterated and covered over. And this is done in the name of a "universal" and "value-free" "science of history"—historical materialism—on which the scientism of socialism is grounded.

But is such a "science of history" possible? Is this not colonialism in the realm and guise of theory? Are not the people of Africa struggling to overcome precisely this—on all levels, including the theoretic—and to establish their own autonomous initiative and self-standing freedom?[13] These are questions which do not occur to Nkrumah, and given his Marxist-Leninist paradigm, cannot occur to him as legitimate and important questions of and for theory.

It will not do to transpose European conceptions onto the African situation since this would not allow the diverse peoples of Africa their own self-standing self-determination. Any and all pre-established frameworks will not reflect the autonomous and historical self-institution that is necessary if Africa is to be free. As Aimé Césaire forcefully points out:

> I never thought for a moment that our emancipation could come from the right—that's impossible . . . our liberation placed us on the left, but [we] . . . refused to see the black [African] question as simply a social [economic] question . . . after all we are dealing with the only race which is denied even the notion of humanity.[14]

According to these eloquent words of the founding poet of *Négritude,* the question of African freedom is not "simply a social [economic] question." Rather, it is a historic, ontic, and ontological question aimed at opening up the originative historic ground on which, in Africa, the social and political—the *polis* as the historic space of the public realm, to paraphrase Heidegger—can be established in freedom, that is, within the context of contemporary African historical existence. In other words, the possibility of African freedom presupposes an open site which is "the historical place, the there *in* which, *out* of which, and *for* which history happens"[15] from within the historicalness of the African situation.

This suggests that the African struggle for freedom cannot, as does the European Left, simply presuppose and start *only* from the political and historic legacy established by the European eighteenth-century bourgeois Liberal Democratic revolutions. Africa, properly speaking, is not heir to this heritage. In other words, the non-European world as a whole, properly speaking, is not interior to the originative historic ground on which the eighteenth-century bourgeois Liberal Democratic revolutions are grounded.

The heritage of the Enlightenment is for us a borrowed inheritance. We share in it only insofar as we are colonized and neocolonized members of *its* modern European-dominated world and have been drastically affected—incorporated by conquest—into its development and globalization. Sharing in this legacy in this way, our aim is to destroy and go beyond this European-dominated disclosure of the present—the historic space in which the battles of the Left are fought and grounded and its hopes and aspirations nourished. Our purpose is not, as it is for the European Left, aimed at fulfilling the "emancipatory" *telos* of European history, whatever that might be. Rather, from within our own African historicalness—which encompasses direct colonialism, its demise, and neocolonialism—we have to quarry and carve out a liberating and edifying political tradition.

Our efforts are aimed at reclaiming our histories, whose destruction and obliteration is presupposed by all the political shades—including the Left—of European modernity. Thus, to extract and uncover that which is covered over by the historicity of European modernity, it is necessary, conversely, to undermine and cover over the historic ground of European modernity. It is only thus that we will simultaneously transgress and appropriate this disclosure.

The European Left basically fights for politico-economic demands within an already established history. It is located and arises out of a tradition and history which explicitly presupposes the destruction of our traditions and histories. At its best, the Left and the struggles of the European working class are political and economic manifestations of the most radical possibilities proper to the historicalness of European modernity. All this, to be sure, does not take into account the colonized non-European. Or rather, it takes account of the colonized by presupposing the necessity of colonial conquest—as a harsh historical prerequisite for the dialectical completion and fulfillment of "human" (i.e., European) freedom globally.

The first few pages of the *Communist Manifesto*, for example, triumphantly recognize and celebrate the worldwide victory of the European bourgeoisie over non-European cultural and historical formations. For Marx, European feudal society is the zenith of, and essentially the same as, non-European traditional social formations. It is for this reason that in the *Manifesto* he dismisses both of these disparate social organizations of life in the same breath.

From these well-known pages, it is clear that for Marx and the European Left as a whole the class war of the proletariat is waged and historicized on the terrain of a homogenized historicalness constituted by the worldwide hegemonic power of the West. Just as European feudalism had to be supplanted by the modern European bourgeoisie,

in like manner, the emancipation of the international proletariat—
and thus of "humanity"—requires the displacing of traditional non-
European social formations by Westernized indigenous societies.
Marx's "historical logic" is impeccable! As he tells us, "philosophy is
the head of" communist or human "emancipation and the *proletariat*
is its *heart*."[16] The poetry of these words notwithstanding, it has to
be noted that "philosophy" here refers to European thought and more
strictly to German Idealism, and "proletariat" refers to the European
and more strictly to the French and German working classes. Thus is
Europe—or certain aspects of its social and historical existence and
thought—globalized.

The class war of the proletariat is, furthermore, advantageously
conditioned and, in turn, it beneficially stimulates the export of capital
and European global dominion. It is within the scope and confines of
this historicalness that the European proletariat attempts to historicize
itself, that is, to replace the bourgeoisie and inherit its cultural-historical legacy. To inherit and radically transform/transcend, this is the basic
and unifying theoretic self-understanding of the European proletariat
articulated by the various strands of the Marxist tradition—but always
from within the colonialist parameters and presuppositions of European cultural and historic hegemony.

The fundamental aim of the African struggle for freedom, on the
other hand, is to disclose an autochthonous tradition and history of
politico-economic struggles interior to itself. The African struggle is
focused on dethroning the European-dominated present, within which
the Left functions and feels at home, from within and out of the
indigenous historicality of its own historicalness, its concrete political
and cultural existence.

To autochthonously overcome the indigence of our indigenous political and historic existence—created and perpetuated by European colonialism and neocolonialism—is the basic and most fundamental historic task of the African struggle for freedom. Thus, in order to be
true to itself, the struggle for African freedom has to begin by undermining and destructuring the historic ground on which the political discourse of the European Left unfolds. This, furthermore, is not a question of tactics or political expedience that could be avoided or
circumvented, but a question of confronting and being *true* to the
concrete historic situation of Africa.[17]

Even in post-colonial Africa, the struggle against neocolonialism is
a struggle aimed and focused on disclosing the historico-political
ground on which an African political tradition can be instituted within

the context of the present. To be sure, and this cannot be overemphasized, the aim is *not* to return to some "true," "uncontaminated," "original," African *arche*—as if this were possible or even desirable—but to make possible the autonomous and thus authentic self-standing historicity of African existence in the context of the modern world. It is this concrete awareness of our situation that we must constantly cultivate and preserve against the seductive "universalistic" rhetoric of the European Left. This much Nkrumah fails to do.

Hence, in addition to expanding—through our contributions—and appropriating the European heritage of the Left, the struggle for African freedom at a more fundamental level is aimed at overcoming European dominance and reclaiming the politico-historic space of African existence which has been obliterated by European colonialism. It is in this fundamental respect, then, that the struggle for African freedom is not merely or simply a social, economic, or political "question" of the Left. To be true to its own historicalness, the African struggle has to institute an emancipatory tradition and discourse within which the political struggle—the struggle for African freedom—can realize itself. At its fundament, therefore, the struggle for African freedom is an exploration of the interrupted historicalness of Africa and of the ways in which the historicity of this African historicalness can be reclaimed and politically established.[18] This, as we shall see in chapter 4, is the emancipatory project that informs and structures Fanon's and Cabral's thinking.

Nkrumah's failure consists in his incapacity to think through this crucial and enigmatic dimension of the problem. The specificity and distinctive complexity of the African situation escapes him. He views the question of African freedom in strict economic Marxist-Leninist terms and thus reduces the struggle to a question of economic-political control. Once reduced in this manner, the African struggle for freedom is then subsumed within the basic structure of European social, political, and economic concerns. It becomes merely a European problem in the "tropics," which thus requires European solutions which have been "properly" adapted to it. But can such adaptations be "properly" adopted without risking the recolonization and indigence of the indigenous populace? What is the criterion and ground of the "propriety" of the "proper" in this context?

The African philosopher Paulin J. Hountondji points out that Nkrumah's thought vacillates between an "early" Africanist phase and a "later" Marxist-Leninist period. By presenting what he calls a "historicist" reading of Nkrumah's work as a whole, Hountondji argues that the "later" Nkrumah endorsed the Marxist-Leninist thesis that the struggle in Africa is nothing more than the class struggle of Western societies extended to the international arena.[19] Being a Marxist-Leninist himself, Hountondji presents the above as a positive development or maturation of Nkrumah's thought. Thus, Hountondji shares in Nkrumah's failure to grasp the specificity and distinctive particularity of the African situation.

Hountondji deprecates the earlier works of Nkrumah not on technical-philosophical grounds, but because they intend—no matter how inadequately—to think African problems from within the horizon of an Africanist perspective. In this respect it is Nkrumah's self-consciously philosophical work, *Consciencism* (1964), which is strongly attacked.[20]

The inherent contradictions of Hountondji's position are obvious however when he writes that

> it must not be forgotten that later he [Nkrumah] more and more openly declared his allegiance to scientific socialism, that is to Marxism-Leninism, though, of course, without in any way repudiating the authentic African cultural tradition.[21]

Such a statement is nothing more than a futile attempt to square the proverbial circle, since to subscribe to Marx's thought understood as "scientific socialism" or Marxism-Leninism, one necessarily subscribes to an evolutionary developmental metaphysics of history—historical materialism—that places Africa at the lowest rung of an evolutionary ladder of development and which fulfills *its* "objective" and singular "human" *telos* in the historic eventuation of European modernity.

In such a perspective—given the metaphysical structure and logic of the discourse—one necessarily (good intentions notwithstanding!) subordinates Africa to Europe and "solves" African problems by imposing European developmental "formulas," contrived and generated out of the singular historic experience of European modernity. This approach does nothing more than replace the colonialist or neocolonialist yoke with the yoke of the Commisar, armed with "scientific socialism," who tries to play out and replicate in Africa the European historic and developmental experience "properly adapted" to the tropics. In these efforts the good-hearted Comrade Commissar does nothing more than prolong and "properly adopt"—in spite of himself and in a new form—European colonialism.

In view of the above then, "scientific socialism" or Marxism-Leninism is, in the non-European world, a ruthless formula of development.

But what does "development" mean in this context? No more and no less than the imposition of Western ways and attitudes under the guise of liberation or "science." To paraphrase Heidegger, "development" is the global *Ge-stell* (en-framing) of modern technology playing itself out and being manifested as the perpetuation of European modernity's cultural and technological dominance of the Earth.[22] It is this *Ge-stell* of European dominance, manifested as the "neutrality" and "objectivity" of science and technology, that Africa must overcome in order to reclaim and carve out the existential, historical, and political space in which to ground its freedom.

In what has been said thus far, we have rendered the Marxist-Leninist interpretation of Marx's thought—namely, "scientific socialism," endorsed by Nkrumah and Hountondji—questionable in terms of the "prior question" of African freedom.[23] It is therefore necessary at this point to examine the polemical counterposition against which the views of the above two authors are articulated. We thus turn to the *Africanité* or African Socialism of Senghor—the main polemical opponent of the two thinkers we have examined thus far. But what exactly is their attitude to Senghor?

For Hountondji, Senghor's *Africanité* is nothing more than a sustained effort to avoid the political questions of the anti-colonial struggle. In contrast to Aimé Césaire, who, according to Hountondji, uses *Négritude* for political ends, Senghor is engaged in the systematic elaboration of "artificial cultural problems."[24] Hountondji's critique of Senghor is basically an extension of his critique of the ethnographic and documentary orientation in African philosophy. Senghor is numbered first among the secular Ethnophilosophers. *Africanité,* along with the work of Kagame, Mbiti, and Ethnophilosophy as a whole, is—except for Temples's work—part of the mystifying and mystified body of literature that goes by the name "African philosophy."[25] In other words, Hountondji's critique of Senghor is a specification of his broader critique of Ethnophilosophy since Senghor himself, by his explicit allegiance, is an Ethnophilosopher.

In like manner for Nkrumah, Senghor—in contrast to Julius Nyerere for example, who is also an advocate of African socialism—formulates at the foundation of his notion of African socialism a "metaphysics of knowledge"—*Africanité*—which is fundamentally antithetical to "scientific socialism."[26] Thus, when in *Class Struggle in Africa* (1970) Nkrumah writes that the African bourgeoisie "for the most part slavishly" follows its European counterpart with the exception of "certain ideologies which have developed specifically within the African context

. . . the most typical [of which] is the bogus conception of 'négritude,' " without a doubt, he has Senghor's idea of *Africanité* in mind.[27]

A few years earlier, Nkrumah had denounced the very idea of an "African socialism," and referring to Senghor rejected all historico-cultural particularity, embracing "scientific socialism" which he categorically affirmed is grounded on universal principles.[28] In " 'African Socialism' Revisited" (1966) and in "The Myth of the 'Third World' " (1968), Nkrumah systematically opposed any form of distinctiveness or historic particularity. For him, such a thing as "African Socialism" is not possible, as if there could be a "socialism peculiar to Africa. . . . In fact there is only one true socialism: scientific socialism."[29]

It is imperative to emphasize that, in rejecting Senghor's particularism (*Africanité*), Nkrumah and Hountondji reject all cultural-historic distinctiveness. And yet, without batting an eye they endorse "scientific socialism": as if this perspective was devoid of any distinctiveness and cultural-historic specificity. As if, in other words, this particular perspective and the historic ground (European modernity) on which it stands and in which it is grounded were isomorphic with "human existence" in the singular. As if, that is, European modernity, properly speaking, spelled the "true" humanity of the human *as such!*

In order to firmly grasp the consequences of the spell of European modernity, let us examine one last passage from Nkrumah's " 'African Socialism' Revisited," a document that, unlike some earlier works of Nkrumah, is fully endorsed by Hountondji.

> Socialism depends on dialectical and historical materialism, upon the view that there is only one nature subject in all its manifestations to natural laws and that human society is, in this sense, part of nature and subject to its own laws of development.
>
> It is the elimination of fancifulness from socialist action that makes socialism scientific. To suppose that there are tribal, national or racial socialisms is to abandon objectivity in favour of chauvinism.[30]

In the above two passages, as in previous ones, by renouncing all cultural-historic particularity in the name of a "universalistic" socialism which is "scientific," Nkrumah surreptitiously universalizes European modernity—the cultural-historic "tribal, national, or racial" ground privileged and valorized by "dialectical and historical materialism."

In endorsing the abstract universality of dialectical and historical materialism Nkrumah is in effect and inadvertently (in the guise of this "abstractness") doing nothing more than flag-waving for Europe. Thus, through Nkrumah and Hountondji—and in spite of their sincere African cultural nationalism—speaks the nineteenth-century evolutionist and colonialist scientism of Friedrich Engels, the lifelong friend and systematic vulgarizer of Marx's work.[31]

To "suppose" that there is *a* position beyond *all* positions isomorphic and coterminous with reality/Being *as such* is fancifulness to end all fancy! This is, at the level of rhetoric, the theoretic birth place of Stalinism and of the leftist dictatorships of contemporary Africa. It is the delirium of a scientistic metaphysics in which Nkrumah and Hountondji are totally engulfed. In the context of the historic subjugation of Africa by Europe the metaphysics of this Eurocentrism (*scientistic universalism*) is nothing more than colonialism in the realm and in the guise of theory.

Let us now turn to the contrary perspective articulated by Senghor, which basically is an Ethnophilosophical position grounded on an *essentialist particularism.* As should be clear by now, the contrary perspectives of Nkrumah and Senghor anticipate and lay the thematic ground for the debate in contemporary African philosophy, which was outlined in the introduction to this study. As we shall see, these two contradictory positions implicitly share a single Eurocentric metaphysics. In the process of probing Senghor's position, I will expose this hidden metaphysical confluence behind the apparent surface political antagonism. Ultimately, as I have already argued in the introduction, both of these parallel positions suffer from a failure to think through the concrete historicity of the contemporary African situation.

II

Let us begin then by looking at how Senghor defends himself against his Marxist-Leninist detractors.

> Young African intellectuals who have read Marx carelessly and who are still not altogether cured of the inferiority complex given them by the colonizers, criticize me for having reduced the African mode of knowledge to pure emotion, for having denied that there was an African "rationality" and an African technology. They must have read what I have written as carelessly as they had read the scientific socialists. It is a fact that there is a white European civilization and a black African civilization. The question is to explain

their differences and the reasons for these differences, which my opponents have not yet done.[32]

To be sure, the Marxist-Leninists have, in their own way, answered this question. For them it is *not* a question of a "white" or a "black" civilization marked—on the foundational level of ontological description—by a qualitative difference in kinds of human existence. Rather, for the Marxist-Leninists it is a question of the singular and quantitatively uniform sequential unfolding of the world-historical dialectical symbiosis of man and nature.[33]

What Senghor sees as a qualitative difference in kinds of "civilization" between differing human groups—Indo-European, on the one hand, and Arab-Berber and Negro-African, on the other—the Marxist-Leninist explicates as a quantitative regression or progression, an underdevelopment or development, in the evolution of the sequential and ontologically proper relation of man to nature. This relation—the technical control of nature—is ordered according to the singular dictates of the historical dialectic and of structural transformation. The technical control of nature, or the lack thereof, is therefore, for the Marxist-Leninist, the singular and "true" yardstick by which the progression or regression of human groups and humanity as a whole is historically gauged and tabulated. But can such "things" as the progression or regression of human groups be measured without prejudging the evidence in the very act of tabulating it?

As we have already seen in our discussion of Nkrumah and Hountondji, this Eurocentric metaphysical isomorphism, this *scientistic universalism,* in the guise of "universality" and "objectivity," surreptitiously universalizes Europe and subordinates Africa. Let us now turn to Senghor, and see how he answers the "prior question" of African freedom: What are the people of Africa trying to free themselves from and what are they trying to establish?

As already indicated, for Senghor, "there is a white European civilization and a black African civilization." It is in explaining and grasping the ontological grounds for this difference that Senghor answers the "prior question" of African freedom. The terms "white" and "black" or Indo-European, on the one hand, and Berber-Arab and Negro-African, on the other, are not merely exterior racial designations. Rather, this taxonomic ordering of human kinds is, for Senghor, the ground on which the ontological difference, essentiality, and complementarity of human races and civilizations is grounded.[34]

In concluding his talk, "Constructive Elements of a Civilization of

African Negro Inspiration" (1959, Rome) at the Second Congress of
Negro-African Writers and Artists, Senghor observed that new "autonomous or independent States are being born in Negro Africa" and
that

> freedom without consciousness is worse than slavery. . . . The most
> striking thing about the negro peoples who have been promoted to
> autonomy or independence, is precisely the *lack of consciousness*
> of most of their chiefs and their disparagement of Negro-African
> cultural values.[35]

The question of African freedom resolves itself, for Senghor, into the
question of how we are to "integrate *Negro-African values*" into the
process of gaining independence. "There is no question," says Senghor,
"of reviving the past, of living in a Negro-African museum; the question
is to inspire this world, *here and now,* with the values of our past."[36]
But what are these values? As Senghor had pointed out in, "The Spirit
of Civilization or the Laws of African Negro Culture" (1956, Paris),
a central text presented at the First Congress of Negro-African Writers
and Artists, these values are what characterize the humanity of the
human in Negro-African existence.

The Negro-African has an ontological kinship, affinity, or bond with
nature that is absent from European humanity. For Senghor "the Negro
is the man of Nature." As he puts it: "By tradition he [i.e., the Negro]
lives off the soil and with the soil, in and by the Cosmos." He is
"sensual, a being with open senses, with no intermediary between
subject and object, himself at once subject and object." For the Negro-
African, this accord and immediacy to nature is "first of all, sounds,
scents, rhythms, forms and colours; I would say that he is touch, before
being eye like the white European. He feels more than he sees; he feels
himself."[37] This is the Being of the Negro-African—a docile immediacy
in tune with nature. It is this docility and lyrical submissiveness to
nature which Senghor values above all else as the *true* Being of the
Negro-African and he postulates it as the essential defining characteristic in and for the humanity of the human in African existence. This
then is *Africanité!*

Between the European and the African there is a qualitative ontological difference in kinds of rationality. The Negro is "not devoid of
reason, as I am supposed to have said. But his reason is not discursive:
it is synthetic. It is not antagonistic: it is sympathetic. It is another
form of knowledge. The Negro reason does not impoverish things, it

does not mould them into rigid patterns by eliminating the roots and the sap: it flows in the arteries of things, it weds all their contours to dwell at the living heart of the real." In other words: "White reason is analytic through utilization: Negro reason is intuitive through participation."[38] European reason is thus discursive and utilitarian, it aims to control and transform: The "European is empiric, the African is mystic."[39] The European

> takes pleasure in recognizing the world through the reproduction of the object . . . the African from knowing it vitally through image and rhythm. With the European the chords of the senses lead to the heart and the head, with the African Negro to the heart and the belly.[40]

The African

> does not realize that he thinks: he feels that he feels, he feels his *existence,* he feels himself; and because he feels the Other, he is drawn towards the other, into the rhythm of the Other, to be re-born in knowledge of the world. Thus the act of knowledge is an "agreement of conciliation" with the world, the simultaneous consciousness and creation of the world in its indivisible unity.[41]

It is necessary to stress and emphasize that, for Senghor, the above "descriptions" (racist imputations?) of the Negro-African are *not* merely historical and thus contingent characteristics of a particular culture and history at a specific point in time. Rather, just as the Marxist-Leninists present their conception of history as the timeless "truth" of history, in like manner the above "descriptions" are, for Senghor, the abiding nature of differing races and cultures. It is imperative to note here that Senghor is not articulating *a* view; rather, he is allowing himself the honor of being the passive vehicle for the self-articulation of *the* "truth" of human existence *as such.*

Epistemically speaking, of course, one can always ask: Is this humility or arrogance? Or is it arrogance masquerading as humility? In other words, as Senghor puts it: "Nature has arranged things well in willing that each people, each race, each continent, should cultivate with special affection certain of the virtues of man; that is precisely where originality lies."[42] But from what "extra-natural" vantage point does Senghor "sight" this "truth"? This is a question that does not and cannot occur to the philosopher of *Africanité* precisely because, as we shall see, his thinking is enveloped and specified within the Otherness of the Other as projected by Europe's own metaphysical and delusionary self-conception. It is within this Eurocentric projection that *Africanité* is encased and thus essentially constituted.

In this epistemically suspect "view" then, Africa is to "cultivate" its own most intuitive reason and Europe its own most discursive reason! Therein lies the "originality" and the "true"—ontologically speaking—essential complementarity of each. Why does one think of Lucien Levy-Bruhl as one reads these lines? Is it at all possible that Senghor is trying to pass off Levy-Bruhl's racism as *Africanité*?[43]

The European in confronting "the object, the exterior world, nature, the Other. . . . Armed with precision instruments . . . dissects it with a ruthless analysis." The African on the other hand "sympathizes and identifies himself . . . dies to himself in order to be reborn to the Other. He is not assimilated; he *assimilates himself* with the Other. He lives with the Other in symbiosis; he is born again (*con-nâit*) to the Other."[44] The African-Negro's "sympathetic" knowledge of the Other is immediate, as Hegel would say. It is in-born, born-with (*con-nâit*), and direct. It is natural, instinctive, and intuitive. The ontological difference that marks off the Negro-African from the Indo-European is, for Senghor in Hegelian terms, immediacy. It is the *lack* of a self-differentiated conscious freedom, reflective mediacy, and detachment from the object or oneness with nature. Of course, as is well known, such a being for Hegel, properly speaking, could not be human.[45] Humanity, in Hegelian terms, is constituted by a sublated and mediated differentiation of subject (humanity) and object (nature). It is precisely for this "reason" that Hegel, in the introduction to his *Philosophy of History,* places Africa beyond the bounds of human civilization proper.

The values of *Africanité* are: intuitive or tactile spontaneous reason, sensation, sensuousness, instinct, feeling, rhythm, image, creativity, imagination, naturalness, immediacy (athletic prowess? sexualness? animality?). Thus, in art, "the kingdom of childhood where Négritude is King," writes Senghor, shamelessly paraphrasing the racialist and racist Count de Gobineau, we have nothing to learn from Europe.[46] This then is a sampling of Senghor's *Africanité* which he characterizes as the *"sum of the cultural values of the black world."*[47]

I hope my reader will forgive the extensive and incessant quoting of rather offensive material, but the evidence, such as it is, has first to be presented before we can unpack Senghor's internalized and ontologized racism. It is important to begin by noting that all the references given thus far are to occasional papers presented either as positive elaborations—as in 1956 and 1959, and in the paper "Latinity and Négritude" of 1964—or as a polemical defense of this position—as in "Négritude: A Humanism of the Twentieth Century" (1970). The views presented in these occasional papers, however, are not themselves transient positions. They are, as we have noted above, Senghor's measured response to the founding "prior question" of African freedom.

Senghor systematically defends these views in: *On African Socialism* (1961), *The Foundations of Africanité or "Négritude" and "Arabité"* (1967), and in *Prose and Poetry* (1976), an anthology of his work prepared with his active assistance and collaboration. These last three texts are not mere occasional formulations, but substantial articulations of Senghor's position.

Now, after Edward Said's *Orientalism* and V. Y. Mudimbe's *The Invention of Africa*, it is difficult to seriously engage Senghor's *Africanité*, for it is nothing more than the ontologizing of Eurocentric ideas projected and presented as the African's own self-conception. Said and Mudimbe present a systematic and critical unpacking of the prejudgments that constitute these ideas. Senghor, on the other hand, like a good Orientalist, Orientalizes, or better still, Africanizes the African.[48] And all this in the name of African freedom.

Without critically unpacking the negative descriptions of the African—which constitute the Otherness of the Other—offered by the ethnographic and anthropological sources he refers to, Senghor overwhelms his reader with "facts and figures." The Eurocentric prejudgments out of which these "facts and figures" are constructed, however, he does not question. Basing himself on the racialist and racist ethnography of Count de Gobineau, on the nebulous speculations of the Catholic philosopher Teilhard de Chardin, and the colonialist ontologizing of Father Placide Temples, Senghor is happy to construct an African-Negro (and by extension a Berber-Arab) essence.[49] How does Senghor achieve this miraculous marvel? He simply takes negative Eurocentric descriptions and presents them as positive Negrocentric manifestations of an ontological difference in and for the being of the Negro-African.

As far back as 1952, in *Black Skin, White Masks*, Fanon had convincingly argued that the European "sees" the Negro-African and pastes on him an Image of Otherness that needs to be critically peeled off and rejected.[50] Quite to the contrary, Senghor pastes and repastes, and thus perpetuates this very image. He uncritically presents racist Eurocentric descriptions as positive manifestations of the African's Being-in-the-world.

Senghor does not see that these descriptions are always structured within parameters which are internal to an evaluative prejudgment that takes Europe as its measure and standard. Within the bounds of this biased gauge—the Eurocentric descriptions which Senghor appropriates—the African is always already the inferior, the Other of Europe, since Europe is, *de facto* and *de jure,* the norm. Or as Said puts it:

> Can one divide human reality, as indeed human reality seems to be genuinely divided, into clearly different cultures, histories, traditions, societies, even races, and survive the consequences humanly? By surviving the consequences humanly, I mean to ask whether there is any way of avoiding the hostility expressed by the division, say, of men into "us" (Westerners) and "they" (Orientals [or Africans]). For such divisions are generalities whose use historically and actually has been to press the importance of the distinction between some men and some other men, usually towards not especially admirable ends. When one uses categories like Oriental [*Africanité*] and Western as both the starting and the end points of analysis, research, public policy . . . the result is usually to polarize the distinction—the Oriental becomes more Oriental, the Westerner more Western—and limit the human encounter between different cultures, traditions, and societies.[51]

Senghor's strategy for overcoming the consequences of this division "humanly" is to ontologically sanction it. In other words, when Senghor encounters those famous (infamous?) pages of Hegel's introduction to the *Philosophy of History,* where Hegel "characterizes" the primeval savagery of the African Negro, he would have to agree with all the basic descriptions—minus some "minor" outrageous allusions to cannibalism—and go on to properly redescribe and appropriate the negative attributes that Hegel pastes on the Negro-African as positive endowments of *Africanité.*[52] To be sure, as Fanon points out—squarely confronting Said's larger and more important question—the only way to overcome this division and its consequences "humanly" is to recognize "the reciprocal relativism of different cultures, once the colonial status is irreversibly excluded."[53]

Senghor's blindness to the racism of his sources is grounded in a shared metaphysics. Said points out that the Orientalist's thinking or, in terms of our present discussion, Senghor's thinking, the thinking of the philosopher of *Africanité,* of the "Platonic Idea"[54] of Negro-ness, is grounded on idealized structures. As Anwar Abdel Malek puts it:

Thus one ends with a typology—based on a real specificity, but detached from history, and, consequently, conceived as being intangible, essential—which makes of the studied "object" another being with regard to whom the studying subject is transcendent; we will have a homo Sinicus, a homo Arabicus (and why not a homo Aegypticus, etc.), a homo Africanus, the man—the "normal man," it is understood—being the European man of the historical period, that is, since Greek antiquity.[55]

In other words, the Orientalist's image of the Otherness of the Other, or in our case, Senghor's conception of *Africanité* is internally structured and overdetermined by the metaphysical assumption that the European is, properly speaking, "unlike the Oriental [or Negro-African]," the "true human being." This, as Said affirms, is the purest example of "dehumanized thought."[56] It is dehumanized because this kind of "thinking" is ultimately grounded on nothing other than brute force and violence, since all the images and conceptions of "homo" Sinicus, Aegypticus, Arabicus, Africanus, etc., including Senghor's *Africanité,* are framed and inaugurated out of the politico-historic horizon of a violently imperialistic Europe.

The Orientalist, as Said tells us without querying this central point further,[57] and the European colonialist—from whom Senghor inherits all of his descriptions of *Africanité*—start from the belief that European existence is the "true" and "proper" manifestation of humanity in its concrete developmental self-realization. This belief is grounded on the metaphysical delusion, interior to their culture, that Europe's specific particularity is the "true" and "proper" actuality of human existence as such. But on what metaphysical criterion does this claim rest? What is the ground of this Eurocentric isomorphism? In other words, what is the ground on which is established the "propriety" of the "proper" in this gratuitous metaphysical European self-evaluation? Strange as it may seem, it is Senghor—the champion of *Africanité* and Negroness—who will supply us with the positive metaphysical ground for this bogus Eurocentric claim.

As Senghor tells us in *The Foundations of Africanité,* Dr. Leakey discovered in 1963, in the Olduwai Valley of Tanzania, the remains of *Homo habilis.* This is a discovery of "capital importance" precisely because

Homo habilis is the first *Homo faber,* more simply, the first man worthy of the name to emerge from animality, since it is at his level and mixed with his fossilized bones that the earliest pebble tools were discovered. These seem to have been made by him.[58]

It is crucial that we properly grasp what Senghor says of this discovery. *Homo habilis* is "the first man worthy of the name to emerge from animality." Why? Because it is "at his level" that we find "the earliest pebble tools." In other words, the humanity of the human in the *habilis* (handy) is grounded on the originative fact that it is the earliest manifestation of man the maker—*Homo faber*. It is "pebble tools," early and rudimentary manifestations of a manipulative-pragmatic orientation to nature, that confirm the humanity of the human in *Homo habilis.*

In other words, "making" is here understood not as artistic creativity, but as pebble tools, elementary and rudimentary products of a utilitarian-pragmatic orientation aimed at the instrumental use and manipulation of nature. The question then becomes: On what kind of reason or rationality is such a utilitarian and pragmatic orientation based? Is it discursive or intuitive? The import of this question lies in the fact that, for Senghor, Leakey's discovery established the initial originative point of emergence of humanity proper out of the realm of "animality." This, furthermore, was provoked and called forth by the act of "making" grounded on a technical and instrumental orientation to the natural environment, i.e., on discursive reason.

As Senghor tells us, reaffirming what we have already seen in his occasional publications, the

> Indo-European and Negro-African were placed at the antipodes, that is to say, at the extremes of objectivity and subjectivity, of discursive reason and intuitive reason [and he has] . . . advocated the symbiosis of these different but complementary elements.[59]

As has already been noted, the Negro-African's mode of knowledge is intuitive, and as such, it is the extreme manifestation of "subjectivity." On the other hand, Indo-European reason is discursive, and as such, it is the extreme manifestation of "objectivity," aimed at the instrumental control of nature. Hence, based on what has been said thus far, it is Indo-European humanity which, properly speaking, is the embodiment of "true" humanity *as such*. This is so precisely because *its* reason—discursive reason—is the kind of reason which first extricates and disentangles the humanity of the human out of the realm of "animality."

To be sure, as Senghor consoles us, humanity as such, at some level or other, shares in "discursive reason." No "civilization can be built," he tells us, "without using discursive reason and without techniques." In fact, "every ethnic group possesses *different aspects of reason* and all the virtues of man, but *each has stressed only one aspect of reason, only certain virtues.*"[60] In other words, the "aspect" which is "stressed" in the Indo-European and which specifies its *particular humanity* is that which, properly speaking, institutes and grounds the humanity of the human *as such.* The particularity of the particular in European humanity—unlike the specific particularity of the African—is coincident with the universality of the universal. Europe is thus, properly speaking, the "truth" of humanity. But then, when Senghor advocates the "symbiosis" and complementarity of these two different kinds of reason, is he not advocating the subordination of Africa to Europe on metaphysical grounds?

On African Socialism is the text in which Senghor engages in an extended and systematic confrontation with Marxism-Leninism. The overall orientation of this text is to advocate a socialism in tune with the Being of the Negro-African, a socialism which takes into account the nature-immersed Being of the African-Negro.[61] But, given what has been said thus far, one might well ask: Is this not a socialism of inferiority and subordination?

Senghor tells us that the European "always separated himself from the object in order to know it. He kept it at a distance . . . he always killed it and fixed it in his analysis to be able to use it in practice."[62] The Negro-African, on the other hand, is "like one of those Third Day Worms, a pure field of sensations."[63] In other words, "European reasoning is analytical, discursive by utilization; Negro-African reasoning is intuitive by participation."[64] The one is aggressive, it grasps and controls; the other is docile and harmoniously in tune with nature. And yet, the above notwithstanding, for Senghor the *true* and

> proper characteristic of Man [as such] is to snatch himself from the earth . . . to escape in an act of *freedom* from his "natural determinations." It is by liberty that man conquers nature and reconstructs it on a universal scale, that man realizes himself as a god; this is freedom.[65]

What then of *"ceux qui n'ont jamais rien invente . . . qui n'ont jamais rien explore . . . qui n'ont jamais rien dompte,"* but who abandon themselves *"a l'essence de toute chose"*?[66] Can we really say "Eia"

(Hurray!) to those who are still immersed within the bowels of nature and without deception, duplicity, or hypocrisy hold on to the above conception of freedom?

Doesn't Senghor—on his own terms—surreptitiously privilege discursive/European in contradistinction to intuitive/Negro-African reason? What is meant here by the "proper characteristic of Man"? Is it not in terms of what is "proper to Man" that European philosophy systematically legitimated the conquest and subjugation of Africa and the non-European as "savage." For now all we need to note is that for Senghor, in perfect accord with Hegel: the *savage* is he whose humanity is within the bounds of "natural determinations,"[67] he whose humanity is *not* manifested as the systemic conquest of nature, he who does not, in Senghor's words, "snatch himself from the earth."

In other words, *Africanité*—on its own terms—describes the humanity of the human in Negro-African existence as *primitive savagery*. As we noted with Said and Abdel Malek, all of the descriptions that constitute *Africanité* are composed and inwardly determined in contradistinction to the "proper characteristic of Man"—the humanity of the human as historically epitomized by Europe. As should be obvious by now, it is discursive reason which is the ground for that which is the "proper characteristic of Man." Thus, for Senghor, appearances notwithstanding, the "propriety" of the "proper"—that which is the "norm" for humanity as a whole—is established by the historicalness of European existence. We have now come full circle: We are again in the company of Marxism-Leninism.

In our discussion of Nkrumah and Hountondji, we saw how the Marxist-Leninist position metaphysically privileges European modernity by obliterating the specificity and particularity of the African in the name of a *universalistic scientism*. Senghor achieves an analogous result by constructing the Being of the African—*Africanité*—out of the Otherness of the Other projected by Europe and internally demarcated by it as the negative exterior of Europe's own positive interiority.

Senghor's *essentialist particularism* arrogates to the African a difference which is (in spite of Senghor's "good" intentions) the ground for inferiority and servitude. Nkrumah and Hountondji on the other hand, "objectively" place the African on the lowest rung of an evolutionary-metaphysical ladder, itself constructed out of the generative biases and prejudgments that ground the specificity of European modernity. In both of the above "opposed" positions this is a failure by default. It is the incapacity to think through the concrete historicity of contemporary African existence.

The contrary perspectives of Nkrumah and Senghor thematically anticipate, within the discourse of the African liberation struggle, the sterile dispute of Ethnophilosophy and its "critical" critics. As Okolo has observed, "on the strictly philosophic plane" this "is the expression of a problematic that oscillates between a naive Ethnophilosophy and an unproductive criticism."[68] In this context "unproductive criticism" describes not only the current status of debate in African philosophic thought but also and more important, the neocolonial impotence which pervades the continent as a whole and which has been dramatized so well in the films and novels of Sembene Ousmane.[69]

In concrete political terms, this failure at "opposite extremes" manifests itself identically as the impotence of neocolonial Africa.[70] It is the enigma of this *xala* (impotence in Wolof), in the prolonged and acrimonious dispute between Professional and Ethnophilosophy, which encompasses the contemporary discourse of African philosophic thought. As we have seen, what both of these seemingly contrary positions lack is an awareness of their lived historicity and the requisite historicizing of their thought which goes with such an awareness.

As Heidegger has insightfully observed, appropriating Count Yorck's remarks:

> Just as physiology cannot be studied in abstraction from physics, neither can philosophy from historicality—especially if it is a critical philosophy. Behaviour and historicality are like breathing and atmospheric pressure . . . it seems to me methodologically like a residue from metaphysics not to historicize one's philosophizing.[71]

In this chapter, in looking at Nkrumah and Senghor, I have located the ground for the historically sightless debate of contemporary African philosophy in the theoretic legacy of the African liberation struggle. This debate has thus far dominated the discourse of African philosophic thought. Beyond this dispute, however, African philosophy needs to engage the unending strife and the debilitating *xala* of our post-colonial present. In view of the above, and taking my cue from the historically astute perspectives of Fanon and Cabral, in the following two chapters I will explore the violence (chapter 3) and the emancipatory possibilities (chapter 4) of the post-colonial African situation.

How our explorations, thus far, have steered and guided us in this direction should by now be clear. For, ultimately, to "historicize one's philosophizing" is to make one's philosophic reflections sensitive to the historicity out of which they originate—that is, to resuscitate and explore the concerns grounded in our own lived historical existence.

3

Colonialism and the Colonized
Violence and Counter-violence

Tribes living exclusively on hunting or fishing are beyond
the boundary line from which real [historical] development begins.

—Karl Marx
From *Introduction to a Critique of Political Economy,*
1857–58

I say, listen to my words and mark them. We have fought
for a year. I wish to rule my country and protect my religion. We have both suffered considerably in battle with
one another. I have no forts, no houses. I have no cultivated fields, no silver or gold for you to take. If the country
was cultivated or contained houses or property, it would
be worth your while to fight. The country is all jungle, and
that is no use to you. If you want wood and stone you can
get them in plenty. There are also ant-heaps. The sun is
very hot. All you can get from me is war, nothing else.

—Sayyid Mohamed Abdille Hassen
Somali anti-colonialist leader 1899–1920
From an "Open Letter to the English People"

Given the violence of Africa's encounter with Europe through which
the "dark" continent was introduced into the modern world, the question of violence should have a central importance for the discourse of
contemporary African philosophy. And yet, to date, African philosophers have not properly dealt with or even engaged the question. To
my knowledge the only texts in Anglophone Africa that directly address

this issue are: a short paper by Kwasi Wiredu titled, "The Question of Violence in Contemporary African Political Thought" (1986); and a slender booklet by Henry Odera Oruka titled, *Punishment and Terrorism in Africa* (1976).[1] Both of these texts are rather formalistic tracts that do not engage, let alone properly explore, the question of violence in the context of the historicity out of which it arises.

Wiredu's paper is a concise tactical discussion of the utility and value of violence, as contrasted to nonviolent methods, in the context of the anti-colonial struggle. But does the question of violence historically pose itself in this way? Oruka's booklet, on the other hand, is an analytic discussion of crime and punishment that advocates leniency and a curative pedagogical approach to villainy. But can the question of punishment be queried without looking at the grounds—political and historical—for the legitimacy of the punishing authority?

In both cases the historicity out of which the question of violence arises in contemporary Africa is silently ignored. This chapter is an attempt to redress this deficiency. Based on Frantz Fanon's seminal reflections on violence, it hopes to engage the question in and out of the historicity of Africa's encounter with Europe.[2] Why so? Precisely because this encounter was, in its very nature inherently violent and had, for the actuality of contemporary Africa, a transfiguring and defining impact.

The importance of this historically attentive approach lies in the fact that it takes its point of departure from a grounding and necessary fact of our contemporary African historicity. This concrete situatedness of our present is the origin of its reflective engagement. In other words, it starts from and grounds itself on the violent inception of its own present enigmatic condition.

In view of the above this chapter will be composed of three sections. The first section will place the question of violence within the historicity of Africa's encounter of Europe. The second section will explore this encounter by utilizing, for this purpose, Fanon's originative discussion of violence in the first section of *The Wretched of the Earth*. The third section will conclude by suggesting the prospect—which will be the central focus of chapter 4—of negating the enduring violence of colonialism and neocolonialism in the consolidation of the concrete possibilities of the African liberation struggle.

I

Aimé Césaire opens his *Discourse on Colonialism* (1955) by noting that interior to the essential constitution of European modernity is the relation with its Other—the colonized non-European world. Césaire observes that

> Europe is unable to justify itself either before the bar of "reason" or before the bar of "conscience"; and that, increasingly it takes refuge in a hypocrisy which is all the more odious because it is less and less likely to deceive.[3]

In referring to "reason" and "conscience" Césaire indicates that he is engaged in an internal and immanent critique. Europe is found wanting on its own terms, by the very criteria it uses to externally evaluate and condemn the humanity of the non-European as uncivilized and primitive.

For Césaire, colonialism and the hypocrisy that is needed to justify it are predicated on "internal reasons" that impel European modernity to "extend to a world scale the competition of its antagonistic economies."[4] In pointing to internal economic reasons, Césaire makes clear that he presupposes a classical Marxist-Leninist analysis of imperialism and colonialism. As is well known, a year later, in conjunction with his resignation from the French Communist Party, he gives us, in addition to the above, a much more substantial and non-Eurocentric reading of the relationship of the colonized to Europe.

In his *Letter to Maurice Thorez* (1956) he asserts, against the universalizing and hegemonic politics of the European Left, that the fundamental concern of the colonized is to retake the initiative of history: to again become historical Being. It is to *negate the negation* of its lived historicalness and overcome the violence of merely being an object in the historicity of European existence that the colonized fights.

Thus, it is the inter-implicative dialectic of this primordial violence, and the counter-violence it evokes, that we need to concretely grasp. For this is the lived historicity out of which the actuality of violence presents itself in the non-European world and thus in contemporary Africa. As Edward Said insightfully observes:

> Imperialism was the theory, colonialism the practice of changing the uselessly unoccupied territories of the world into useful new versions of the European metropolitan society. Everything in those territories that suggested [difference] waste, disorder, uncounted resources, was to be converted into productivity. . . . You get rid of most of the offending human and animal blight . . . you confine the rest to reservations, compounds, native homelands, where you can count, tax, use them profitably, and you build a new society on the vacated space. Thus was Europe reconstituted abroad its

"multiplication in space" successfully projected and managed. The result was a widely varied group of little Europes throughout Asia, Africa, and the Americas, each reflecting the circumstances, the specific instrumentalities of the parent culture, its pioneers, its vanguard settlers. All of them were similar in one other major respect— despite the differences, which were considerable—and that was that their life was carried on with an air of *normality*.[5]

The first act of freedom that the colonized engages in is the attempt to *violently* disrupt the "normality" which European colonial society presupposes. The tranquil existence of the colonizer is grounded on the chaotic, abnormal, and subhuman existence of the colonized. The "new societies" that replicate Europe in the non-European world are built on "vacated space" which hitherto was the uncontested *terra firma* of different and differing peoples and histories.

The dawn and normalcy of colonial society—i.e., the birth and establishment of the modern Europeanized world, as Karl Marx approvingly points out in the first few pages of the *Communist Manifesto*—is grounded on the negation of the cultural difference and specificity that constitutes the historicity and thus humanity of the non-European world.[6] European modernity establishes itself globally by violently negating indigenous cultures. This violence in replication, furthermore, accentuates the regressive and despotic/aristocratic aspects internal to the histories of the colonizing European societies.

In imposing itself Europe cannot keep faith with the central tenets of its own bourgeois democratic heritage. In fact, paradoxically, the colonies are the negation of this heritage in the very act of "duplicating" it. European democracy in the colonies is unabashed fascism.[7] Apartheid South Africa, British Kenya, and French Algeria are paradigmatic examples of this contradiction. In order to verify this observation, all one needs to do is compare the life of the colonized African under European democracies and avowed fascist dictatorships. French Algeria and the Portuguese colonies, British Kenya and Italian Eritrea, despite their many differences and in differing ways, are identical in their respective disparagement of the indigenous historicity.

In all of this, it has to be noted that Europe—fascist or democratic— undertook the domination of the world and Africa not in the explicit and cynical recognition of its economic-colonialist interest, but in the delusion that it was spreading civilization and beneficially Christianizing the globe. For the colonialist consciousness, colonialism is an altruistic and generous self-sacrificing project. At least, as Albert Memmi tells us, this is the image the colonialist wants to believe and wants others to believe about him.[8]

In fact, as Mudimbe has correctly pointed out, the colonizing venture of Europe in Africa has always been and cannot but be a twofold mission of spiritual and earthly dominion disguised, even to itself, as an evangelic and civilizing mission to the world.[9] In other words:

> Missionary speech is always predetermined, preregulated, let us say *colonized*. . . . This is God's desire for the conversion of the world. . . . This means, at least, that the missionary does not enter into dialogue with the pagans . . . but must impose the law of God that he incarnates. . . . God is rightly entitled to the use of all possible means, even violence, to achieve his objectives.[10]

Conveniently, European colonial consciousness saw itself in the image of fulfilling both the demands of God and the requirements of civilized human existence. In colonizing, the missionary—or generally speaking the Christian European—is not violating or transgressing on non-European cultures. Rather, he is realizing divine providence, the mission bestowed on the twelve apostles by Christ: to spread the faith to the four corners of the globe.

Thus, colonial consciousness, in the very act of conquest is itself spellbound by its own spiritual and earthly myths. In Rudyard Kipling's poignant words:

> Take up the white Man's burden—
>   Send forth the best ye breed—
> Go bind your sons to exile
>   To serve your captives' need;
> To wait in heavy harness
>   On fluttered folk and wild—
> Your new-caught, sullen peoples,
>   Half devil and half child.[11]

As Mudimbe's account indicates, and as the above shows, the European takes himself as the norm of human existence *per se* and imposes his own particularity as universal on the non-European who is viewed as "half devil and half child." Notice the clear and clean concurrence of God's work and the exigencies of European expansion. Given this "coincidence," European colonial consciousness, in contrast to the rest of us, cannot but see itself as the vicar of the true revealed faith. The epistemic untenability of this blind belief is the metaphysical ground on which the colonialist project, both in its sacred and secular manifestations, rests. Indeed, it goes without saying, the "devil" has to be exorcized and the "child" has to mature![12]

Elaborating a secular variant of the above from within the engaged discourse of the "materialist conception of history," Karl Marx wrote in 1853:

> England, it is true, in causing a social revolution in Hindustan, was actuated only by the vilest interests, and was stupid in her manner of enforcing them. But that is not the question. The question is, can mankind [in the singular] fulfill its *destiny* [in the singular] without a fundamental revolution in the social state of Asia? If not, whatever may have been the *crimes* of England she was the *unconscious tool of history* in bringing about that revolution. Then, whatever bitterness the spectacle of the crumbling of an ancient world may have for our personal feelings, we have the right, *in point of history* to exclaim with Goethe:
>
> > Should this torture then torment us
> > Since it brings us greater pleasure?
> > Were not through the rule of Timur
> > Souls devoured without measure?[13]

What has to be noted in these lines—which applies not only to India but to the rest of the non-European world as a whole—is that Marx is not blind to the hypocrisy and brutality of British or European rule. In fact he recognizes in detail, in his articles on India, as well as in chapters 26 and 31 of *Capital*, vol. I, the violence upon which European expansion is grounded. In point of "history," however, and in terms of the singular "destiny" of "mankind," the destructive violence of European conquest and expansion are exonerated. This is so precisely because the violence of colonial conquest makes possible a "fundamental revolution in the social state" of the non-European world, i.e., it brings about the forced but necessary and propitious globalization of Europe.[14]

In like manner, reflecting on the socio-economic dialectic internal to European modernity, G. W. F. Hegel wrote in 1821:

> This inner dialectic of civil society [i.e., of European modernity] thus drives it—or at any rate a specific civil society—to push beyond its own limits and seek markets, and so its *necessary* means of

subsistence, in other lands which are either deficient in the goods it has overproduced, or else generally backward in industry.[15]

Colonialist expansion is presented by Hegel as the ideal solution to the internal and inherent (i.e., "necessary") contradictions of European modernity. Thus, territories which do not suffer from the peculiarly modern European problem of "overproduction" are labeled "generally backward in industry" and thereby become the legitimate prey of colonialist conquest. Expansion and "systematic colonization"[16] directed by the state are, in this scenario, the process by which culture and civilization are spread. What is silently left out of this picture is the fact that this globalization of European civilization presupposes and is grounded on the systemic destruction of non-European civilizations.

Like Marx—who is himself, in this respect, Hegel's faithful disciple—but focused on the self-unfolding of *Weltgeist* (world-spirit), Hegel also thinks of humanity and history (in the singular) as the phenomenal manifestation of *Geist* (spirit), and European culture and historicity as the proper and highest illustration of this world-historical process.[17] For Kipling, Marx, and Hegel, in keeping with the critical self-consciousness and self-conception of European modernity, colonialism is seen as a required and necessary step in the unfolding of world history.[18] In this regard the opinions of David Hume and Immanuel Kant, the pivotal precursors of nineteenth-century European thought, are of cardinal importance. For as Hume puts it:

> I am apt to suspect the negroes, and in general all the other species of men (for there are four or five different kinds) to be naturally inferior to whites. There never was a civilized nation of any complexion than white.

In categorical agreement with the above, Kant asserts that

> so fundamental is the difference between the two races of men, and it appears to be as great in regard to mental capacities as in color.[19]

In view of the above, as Father Placide Temples puts it, "our civilizing mission alone can justify our occupation of the lands of uncivilized peoples."[20] Notice the correlation between "occupation"—i.e., unmitigated violence—and Europe's "civilizing mission." Colonial violence sees itself as character-forming chastisement and in this unequivocally adheres to Aristotle's self-serving dictum that "slaves stand even more in need of admonition than children."[21]

Just as for the Greeks the barbarian was the legitimate object of enslavement,[22] in like manner European modernity sees itself as the *Hellas* of the modern age. Colonialist violence justifies itself in its own eyes by its "progressive," "civilizing," and "christianizing" "mission" to the world. As Alan Ryan correctly points out:

> Greek and Roman philosophers thought history was cyclical and repetitive just like any other natural process. . . . The Judeo-Christian tradition was anti-classical in thinking that history had a definite dramatic shape, with a beginning, a middle, and a conclusion. It was the Christian image of history as a three-act play—Fall, Suffering, Redemption—that found its way into Kant's philosophy of history, into Hegel's and eventually into Marx's supposedly empirical and sociological "materialist conception of history."[23]

Non-European cultures are saved from their "fallen" condition of heathenism through the "suffering" of colonialism and can, through this suffering, look forward to a distant future of possible "redemption." In both its secular and religious manifestations, this view does nothing more than universalize the singular historico-cultural particularity of Europe in the name of a metaphysical—earthly or divine—*telos*.

Thus, in the very act of violent conquest, paradoxically, Europe sees itself as serving its "captive's need." Or, not so enigmatically, as Said puts it:

> Images of blacks, of women, of primitives that occur in the nineteenth century are . . . part of the production of these beings as inferior, and hence as dominated [and justifiably so] by the wielders of the . . . discourse about blacks, women, primitives.[24]

This then is the duplicity that Césaire accuses Europe of. For the image of the "primitive" is interior and necessary to Europe's own gratuitous self-conception. This same "image" is, however, also used to justify the violent destruction of the specific humanity of aboriginal peoples which it supposedly describes.

This violence, furthermore—the violence of the "civilizing mission"—is not a violence of mere destruction. Rather, as Césaire reminds us, it is a duplicitous violence that ranks human societies in subordination. Now, beyond this strange deceit, to the non-European, the expansion of Europe is experienced as the unabashed dawn of systematic and organized global violence. This is a violence that closes off the different and differing cultural and historical totalities within which the non-European exists. The "little Europes" throughout Asia, Africa, and the Americas arose out of this primordial colonizing violence.[25]

The un-freedom in which Africa is presently entangled is thus directly rooted in European dominance. This is what Césaire refers to as the "peculiarity of our history, laced with terrible misfortunes which belong to no other history."[26] We need now to ask: How was this violent dawn experienced by the colonized?

In order to properly grasp the sense of this question let us look at two well-known texts of African imaginative production; Chinua Achebe's *Things Fall Apart* (1959) and Cheikh Hamidou Kane's *Ambiguous Adventure* (1962). These texts concisely articulate—from within Anglophone and Francophone Africa, respectively—the existential anguish suffered by those of us who, as part of our cultural and historical heritage, have a colonized past. Beyond the colonizer's self-serving and delusory self-perception, we need now to look at the colonized.

As Achebe puts it, with the advent of European colonialism "things fell apart." The African's mode of life, his indigenous habitat of human existence, was displaced by the violence of the "civilizing mission." Things African were devalued and the African was reduced to slavery. In the fictional recreation of the demise of the Igbo at the hands of the British, Achebe concisely depicts the truth of this tragic moment of our modern African historicity.

Things Fall Apart ends with the suicide of Okonkwo the warrior chief and main character of the novel, and the reduction of the wise Obierika—the respected and prudent elder in this circumstance—to the status of an informant explaining to the Colonial District Commissioner the abominable character of his worthy friend's appalling end.

> "That man [Okonkwo] was one of the greatest men in Umuofia. You drove him to kill himself; and now he will be buried like a dog. . . ." He could not say any more. His voice trembled and choked his words.[27]

The wise Obierika explains what, up to that point, had been clear and in no need of explanation or interpretation. He is both the witness and incarnation of the estrangement in African existence inaugurated by colonial conquest. From within an Africa overwhelmed by Europe he laments, and by his political impotence manifests, the agonized primordial moment of Africa's mortifying enslavement.

Standing at the feet of Okonkwo's dangling cadaver, which represents defeated but unconquered Africa, the District Commissioner contemplates the writing of a book.

> The story of this man who had killed a messenger and hanged himself would make interesting reading. One could almost write a whole chapter on him. Perhaps not a whole chapter but a reasonable paragraph. . . . There was so much else to include, and one must be firm in cutting out details. He had already chosen the title of the book, after much thought: *The pacification of the Primitive Tribes of the Lower Niger.*[28]

The unbending Okonkwo is the "jungle savage,"[29] to borrow Fanon's sarcastic phrase; he exists beyond the pale of "humanity" proper, i.e., the historicity of European conquest. He is the one who refuses the designation "the Primitive Tribes of the Lower Niger," a colonialist designation which presupposes the negation, as primitive, of the indigenous historicity. Or, in Hegelian terms, Okonkwo symbolizes the rejection of the dialectic of colonial enslavement. In being the concrete personification of its own freedom, this consciousness cannot even conceive of the possibility of being the bondsman in Hegel's dialectic of "lordship and bondage." It chooses demise over bondage.

Okonkwo is the consciousness that refuses to barter, or even contemplate the possibility of bartering, its concrete ethical life—i.e., its freedom—for biological existence.[30] Obierika, obversely, is the spiritual forefather of the *assimilado* and the *évolué*—the enslaved.[31] His wisdom is a prudent knowledge, a skill at bartering self-preservation and the default of freedom. On the other hand, in Obierika's remorse for proud Okonkwo's tragic end, we see the demised remains of self-standing Africa inaugurating the moment of reflective thought out of colonial estrangement in the historicity of our present.[32]

In *Ambiguous Adventure,* Kane recounts the story of Samba Diallo, a young Diallobe boy, from French Senegal, who finds himself in a spiritual-cultural *imbroglio* between his traditional Islamic ambience and the imposed materialistic world of the West, which he has partially internalized. The spiritual-cultural crisis that Samba feels and fails to resolve is the conflict around which the narrative is structured. Utilizing this quandary as a metaphor, Kane engages the lived and systemic enigma of colonized existence.

Again the story ends with the death of the central character. The conclusion strongly suggests that the failure to reconcile the imposed modernity of Europe with the enduring traditions of Africa—which kills Samba—will also, ultimately, be the demise of the continent. In all this, the central moment is the moment of conquest and violence. Let us read Kane.

> Strange dawn! The morning of the Occident in black Africa was spangled with smiles, with cannon shots, with shining glass beads. Those who had no history were encountering those who carried the world on their shoulders. It was a morning of accouchement: the known world was enriching itself by a birth that took place in mire and blood.
>
> From shock, the one side made no resistance. They were a people without a past, therefore without memory. The men who were landing on their shores were white, and mad. Nothing like them had ever been known. The deed was accomplished before the people were even conscious of what had happened.
>
> Some among the Africans, such as the Diallobe brandished their shields, pointed their lances, and aimed their guns. They were allowed to come close, then the cannons were fired. The vanquished did not understand. . . .
>
> Others wanted to parley. They were given a choice: friendship or war. Very sensibly, they chose friendship. They had no experience at all.
>
> The result was the same. . . . Those who had shown fight and those who had surrendered . . . they all found themselves . . . checked by census, divided up, classified, labeled, conscripted, administered.
>
> For the newcomers did not know only how to fight. They were strange people. . . . Where they had brought disorder, they established a new order. They destroyed and they constructed.
>
> Thus, behind the gunboats [stood] . . . the new school.[33]

Behind the "gunboats" stands the "new school": the institutional/cultural weapon which will permanently scar and violate the indigenous culture. The sarcasm of Kane's prose illustrates well the sense of terror and bewilderment with which European modernity dawned on Africa.

This "Strange dawn! The morning of the Occident in black Africa" is the primeval violence on which is grounded the quotidian normalcy of colonialism and neocolonialism, of being "checked by census, divided up, classified, labeled, conscripted, administered." Or as Said puts it:

> You get rid of most of the offending human and animal blight . . .
> confine the rest to reservations . . . where you can count, tax, use
> them profitably, and you build a new society on the vacated space.[34]

Europe experienced the dawn of modernity as the age of Enlightenment. In the words of Immanuel Kant, this was the age in which
"man's release from his self-incurred tutelage"[35] was to be actualized.
A century later Africa experienced its entry into this modern *European*
world, not as liberation or enlightenment, but as the painful process
of colonial subjugation. This is how Fanon puts it:

> Conquest, it is affirmed, creates historic links. The new time
> inaugurated by the conquest, which is a colonialist time because
> occupied by colonialist values, because deriving its *raison d'être*
> from the negation of the national time, will be endowed with an
> absolute coefficient. The history of the conquest, the historic devel-
> opment of the colonization and of the national spoilation will be
> substituted for the real time of the exploited. . . . And what is
> affirmed by the colonized at the time of the struggle for national
> liberation as the will to break with exploitation and contempt will
> be rejected by the colonialist power as a symbol of barbarism and
> of regression.
> The colonialist, by a process of thinking which is after all fairly
> commonplace, reaches the point of no longer being able to imagine
> a time occurring without him. His irruption into the history of the
> colonized people is deified, transformed into absolute necessity. Now
> a "historic look at history" requires, on the contrary, that the French
> colonialist retire, for it has become historically necessary for the
> national time in Algeria to exist.[36]

I have quoted extensively from Fanon and earlier from Kane precisely
because they articulate concisely the moments of primordial conflict
of the two contending forces in the colonial encounter. Kane tells us
that where the colonizers "had brought disorder, they established a
new order." They end one order of time and inaugurate a new colonial
order of time.

Using the example of the French in Algeria, Fanon articulates the
obverse of the colonial conquest. Just as the "irruption" of colonialism
"into the history of the colonized" interrupts the historicity of the
indigenous culture, in like manner the reclaiming of the "national
time" is possible only on the demise of colonial temporality. The
clash is thus a conflict of contending and radically noncommensurable

cultural-historical totalities. As Patrick Taylor correctly points out, for Fanon, the demise or destruction of "the colonizer means the beginning of the possibility of a new history for the colonized."[37] The actualization of this possibility is the reclaiming of human existence for both the former colonizer and the colonized. In Hegelian terms, this is the moment of recognition and freedom.

Let us now with Fanon look in greater detail at the nature and phenomenal character of this violent confrontation and its possible resolution. In so doing we will not be using "Fanon as a global theorist *in vacuo*" as Henry Louis Gates, Jr., accuses Edward Said of doing.[38] Rather, our deployment of this violent text, on violence, stems from the actuality and the ferocity of conflict in colonized and neocolonized Africa. This is the concretely situated—historically and politically originative—context out of which Fanon's reflections on violence were first produced.

II

In the opening pages of his seminal work, *The Wretched of the Earth,* Fanon observes that:

> The colonial world is a world cut in two. The dividing line, the frontiers are shown by barracks and police stations. In the colonies it is the policeman and the soldier who are the official, instituted go-between, the spokesmen of the settler and his rule of oppression.[39]

Fanon is describing the colonial situation as it existed and still exists in Africa. In the colonies things are clear-cut, especially in avowedly colonial times, but also in their neocolonial prolongations. The difference is not only one of pigmentation but also of indigenized colonialist methods. Neocolonialism replicates colonial violence—by proxy—between Westernized and non-Westernized natives. Or, as Fanon puts it

> [This] is the antagonism which exists between the native who is excluded from the advantages of colonialism and his counterpart who manages to turn colonial exploitation to his account.[40]

Thus, what is said of the colonial situation *mutatis mutandis* applies with equal force to neocolonial Africa.

On the one hand, you have the colonizer; on the other, the colonized.

These two groups—one of human beings in the process of extending and globalizing their cultural and historical actuality, and the other of *thingified*[41] entities frozen in time and degraded beyond belief—exist as an organic whole in subordination. The colonizer and the colonized each constitute the Other for one another and determine themselves in terms of the Other.

In the metropolis, the socio-economic relations of civil society and the hierarchical structure of the state—i.e., society as an organic and differentiated whole—are maintained in place by a variety of intersecting socio-historical institutions. The national educational system, the heritage of a common history, norms and modes of behavior and moral conduct implicitly accepted by all muffle class conflicts and institute a reality in which the lower classes' antagonism to those in power is channeled through peaceful avenues. Even the militant communist parties of the European working classes are accepted and represent a respectable political position within the confines of European modernity. All these conflicting, and potentially lethal, political perspectives are held in check by the hegemonic power of a common modern European historicity.

As Fanon points out, the "serf is in essence different from the knight but a reference to divine right is necessary to legitimate this statutory difference."[42] Indeed, in Europe social contradictions are mediated. In the medieval age religion served this purpose, and in modern capitalist Europe the liberal abstract discourse of rights and the ideals of "liberty, equality and fraternity," which animated the French Revolution, still fulfill this task. In the colonies, on the other hand, the dialectic of social existence has no middle term, or, to be more precise, this dialectic is mediated by violence. The relation of the colonizer and the colonized is based on brute force.

Colonialism, as Hegel approvingly observes, originates in the violent contradictions of "civil society" and is a desirable way of institutionally externalizing this violence, which is internal and endemic to European modernity.[43] From the inception of the colonial situation—the time of the colonial conquest—the settler and the colonial society in which he exists are established and maintained by force and violence. The colonized is constantly reminded of his place; in this divided world no one can breach the boundaries with impunity. Be it in the presence of the colonialist police, the wealth of the European farms, or the innumerable statues to the heroes of the period of conquest, the colonized is reminded that he is a "native," an outcast in his own land, a conquered person—a *thing* of service in the historicity of the colonizer.

The "native" is maintained—or held down—in his designated inferior position by the tremendous material and intellectual force exerted against him by the settler and the "mother" country. As Fanon observes:

> Their first encounter was marked by violence and their existence together—that is to say the exploitation of the native by the settler—was carried on by dint of a great array of bayonets and cannons. The settler and the native are old acquaintances. In fact . . . it is the settler who has brought the native into existence and who perpetuates his existence.[44]

One has to grasp the force of Fanon's words. The "settler and the native are old acquaintances." The settler maintains and constitutes—brings "into existence"—the "native" as an inferior being. As the embodiment of his own inferiority, and as long as he remains in this position, the native upholds and endures—as if by choice!—the supremacy of the settler. In this mutual relation one is the complement and the ground of the other. The opposite moments of this interimplicative bond necessarily stand or fall together. Master implies slave and slave implies master.

The colonized is the member of a defeated history. But he also knows that his forefathers—those who confronted the original conquest—fought the aggressor and were defeated not because they lacked courage or wisdom but because they lacked cunning and shrewdness. He knows that his history, the process of his communal becoming, was violently interrupted not because it was impotent, but because it failed—as Cheikh Hamidou Kane tells us—to organize and call forth the requisite violence against the original intruders. The colonized is aware at some level that the socio-human habitat—the *ethos* (i.e., the social-historical space) in which his forefathers lived and acted out their historicity, his peculiar experience of Being or existence—was suppressed, not for lack of wisdom, but because of violence and military strength. In this awareness, the colonized sees the colonizer as a brute with nothing to his merit save his strength. This—the colonizer's strength, his violence—he envies.

The settler and the learned experts from the "mother" country—or the elite of the Westernized native ruling class in a neocolonial context—see things differently. As Fanon points out, they speak of brown, yellow, and black multitudes, or of a backward peasantry in a neocolonial setup. They speak of the colonized or of the subjects of neocolonial exploitation in biological terms and declare them to be the antagonist of history. The native, or the neocolonized peasantry, is said to be inferior and to have no appreciation of values. It is in short, "the negation of values" and of all that humanity claims for itself as human.[45] Thus the settler, or the neocolonial elite, has no regrets or qualms of conscience, for he does violence not to human beings, but to strange entities located between humanity and undifferentiated nature.[46]

For the settler, the "native"—just as for the neocolonial elite, the peasant—is a *thing*, a beast of burden. Just as the flora and fauna of the conquered territory or the neocolonial state, the "native," or the neocolonized peasant, as the case may be, is a more or less useful resource, an object of calculative exploitation. In a neocolonial setup this manifests itself as the defensive and reactive animosity of the elite toward the indigenous peasantry. This rancor, furthermore, is much more pronounced and accentuated to the extent that the neocolonial elite, unlike the former colonizers, has to actively and desperately maintain its difference from the indigenous and indigent folk. This is a case of being more Catholic than the Pope! Thus, the neocolonial elite "does not hesitate to assert that 'they [the peasants] need the thick end of the stick if this country is to get out of the Middle Ages.' "[47] As we saw in chapter 1, to progress or "get out of the Middle Ages" here means to replicate and perpetuate the technological *Ge-stell* of European dominance.[48]

The settler recognizes in his own person the indispensable agent of history. The "settler makes history and is conscious of making it."[49] His constant point of reference, furthermore, is European history and it is in terms of this past that he projects a future. Indeed, it is in light of this duplicity that Césaire's critical remarks, with which we opened this chapter, make sense. Césaire, as we noted, charges colonialist Europe with dissimulation precisely because in the name of the universality of values Europe universalizes its own singular particularity. In the colonies, the paradox of this situation manifests itself in the fact that Europe subjugates the native in order to "civilize" and "liberate" or "save" his soul from barbarism. Thus, in the name of democracy, in the non-European world, Europe institutes colonial fascism.

The colonized, on the other hand, knows that he is human and the incarnation of a distinctive civilization. He knows that the values and culture the settler speaks of were established by force and violence. He is aware, and is made aware by the very structure of colonialist society, of:

> The violence with which the supremacy of white values is affirmed and the aggressiveness which has permeated the victory of these values over the ways of life and of thought of the native.[50]

The colonized is not only a defeated person, he is also resentful, since he is forced to accept the illegitimate power of the colonizer. The colonialist is everything, and the native is forced to accept this in silent terror. Thus:

> The immobility to which the native is condemned can only be called in question if the native decides to put an end to the *history of colonization*—the history of the pillage—and to bring into existence the *history of the nation*—the history of decolonization.[51]

This is possible only through the explicit confrontation of the colonizer and the colonized. It is only when the colonized appropriates the violence of the colonizer and puts forth his own concrete counter-violence that he reenters the realm of history and human historical becoming. Out of bitter experience, the colonized learns the truth of the words with which Jean-Jacques Rousseau opens *The Social Contract*: Force has no moral sanction and thus what is taken by violence can, by the same means, legitimately be regained.[52]

It is at this point that the colonized actively realizes, beyond the inertness of resentment, the viability of his own suppressed indigenous historicity. The very possibility of appropriating a liberating violence has thus a therapeutic effect on the consciousness of the colonized. It is at these moments, as Fanon tells us, that

> We must notice in this *ripening process* the role played by the history of the resistance at the time of the conquest. The great figures of the colonized people are always those who led the national resistance to invasion . . . [they] all spring [at these moments] again to life with peculiar intensity in the period which comes directly before action. This is the proof that the people are getting ready to begin to go forward again, to put an end to the *static period begun by colonization* and to *make history*.[53]

The organic metaphor—"ripening"—that Fanon uses is insightful. Just as the seed or fruit in ripening brings out of itself what it inherently is, in like manner the colonized in resisting makes itself what it inherently is—a community of human beings—by effectively negating its thingification and bringing out of itself the historicity that accentuates its thus far thwarted humanity. It is only in the struggle to contest its subjugation that the colonized concretely reactivates its Being as human. The conflict is between stasis (death) and activity (life).

To exist as a human being is to temporalize, but the colonized as colonized only passively *does* time and subsists in a history of which he is not a participant. As Memmi observes, at times even the citizens of free countries feel helpless in the face of the modern machinery of states and governments. They are like pawns in the hands of the politicians, their elected "civil servants." Yet in principle the citizen is a free member of the body politic. Thus in spite of their apathy and skepticism, the free citizens periodically rise up—for example, May 1968, France—and "upset the politicians' little calculations." On the other hand, the colonized

> Feels neither responsible nor guilty nor skeptical, for he is out of the *game*. He is in no way a subject of history *any more*. Of course, he carries its burden, often more cruelly than others, but always as an object. He has *forgotten* how to participate actively in history and no longer even asks to do so.[54]

So far as he is colonized and remains so, he is nothing more than a *thingified* biological organism with specific life functions. These life functions—eating, breathing, defecating, procreating—are secured at the heavy coast of freedom, namely, human existence. The "native" strictly speaking exists only in the realm of nature. In the realm of history he is a nonperson—his master's zombie.

In order to remember and reenter the realm of human historicity, the colonized has to put his situation as a whole in question. This question, furthermore, assumes the character of violent confrontation precisely because the colonized not only wants to be in the "game" but wants to be the author of the rules as well. In confrontation, the colonized reclaims and asserts the humanity of his existence. This is the particularity of his specific historico-cultural experience of existence/Being. It is in this way that the colonized claims his autonomy and freedom, his Being as history.

As Oliva Blanchette puts it:

> man enters into society [history] as he begins to form his own projects in consort with others or, put another way, society [history] in the concrete is constituted by a community of projects.[55]

But colonialism is precisely the complete negation of the "community of projects" which constitute the historicity of the colonized. The colonized, the "native," is forcefully barred from and does not historicize. Rather he endures as a subordinate *thing* in the historicity of the colonizer. The colonized's Being or humanity—the specific cultural, political, and historical difference that constitutes his existence—begins to unfold only in the act of confrontation. This is so precisely because in this violent engagement he affirms his existence by opening up its concrete possibilities.

In struggle and conflict the colonized passes beyond himself—his thingified status of "native"—and claims the freedom to be the being which opens existence out of itself, through and by its engagement with the world.[56] Conflict and violence are not a choice, they are an existential need negatively arising out of the colonial situation which serves as a prelude to the rehumanization of the colonized. As Fanon points out:

> The settler makes history; his life is an epoch, an Odyssey. He is the absolute beginning: "This land was created by us"; he is the unceasing cause: "If we leave, all is lost, and the country will go back to the middle ages." Over against him torpid creatures, wasted by fevers, obsessed by ancestral customs, form an almost inorganic background for the innovating dynamism of colonial mercantilism.

The other side of this divide the

> coiled, plundered creature which is the native provides fodder for the process as best he can . . . and all the while the native, bent double, more dead than alive, exists interminably in an unchanging dream.[57]

In all this what has to be taken note of is the fact that the violence of the colonized is a reactive violence aimed at the primordial violence incarnated in the colonial situation. It is in a desperate attempt to overcome the delirium of the "unchanging dream" that the colonized is forced to live in the confines of a dehumanized existence.

In this regard, the paradigm *par excellence* of the colonized is the domestic servant. The domestic exists as a "domestic" only to the extent that he does not exist as a human being and is implicated in his own non-existence. As Memmi puts it, the domestic is "his master's respectful shadow."[58] He is the act of executing another's will. He does not have a will of his own. The domestic "acts when he is ordered to, he does not speak of himself, he is never anything but a reflection of his master."[59] The domestic is the embodiment of debasement, "a debasement to which he consents" and in this is implicated in forsaking his own humanity.[60]

The situation of the domestic and the colonized is thus inherently—in its very nature—not open to compromises and half-measures. For what is at stake in this inter-implicative dialectic on the level of ontological description is the humanity of the colonized and of the domesticated nonperson. The being of the master necessarily presupposes the nonbeing of the domestic. The only alternative to the above is the violence of resistance. In this context a "nonviolent" resistance is a contradiction in terms precisely because any self-assertive act of the colonized is bound to violate—hence do violence to—the rule and standard or norm of subjugation and domination on which the colonial relation is grounded.

In Marx's famous words, "violence is the midwife" of social change and historical transformation. In the colonial context, violence is a great deal more: it is the avenue through which humanity is reclaimed.

> Decolonization is the veritable creation of new men [i.e., of a new humanity]. But this creation owes nothing of its legitimacy to any supernatural power; the "thing" which has been colonized becomes man during the same process by which it frees itself.[61]

Through and out of this historical process, which is necessarily violent, the "thing" (i.e., the native) reclaims its own humanity. This is a self-reflexive process from which, if exhaustively consummated, the colonized emerges as human. Borrowing a phrase from Hegel, one can say that decolonization, properly speaking, is "the process of its own becoming . . . and only by being worked out to its [very] end is it actual."[62] Fanon's French properly captures and conveys this self-reflexive Hegelian nuance; "*la 'chose' colonisée deviant homme dans le processus même par lequel elle se libere.*"[63] The process of liberation—*le processus même*—is the avenue through which the concept of humanity is adequated to the lived actuality of the decolonized.

Fanon emphasizes the term "thing" (*chose*) precisely because, just as a domesticated animal, the "native" has lost the sense of life and living. The colonized "native" is a thingified entity, just as the domesticated animal is an agricultural resource—a beast of burden. It is only in the process of violent confrontation that life is reappropriated and the colonized reinstitute their humanity.

In this regard, as Patrick Taylor points out, it should be noted that, "[u]nderneath the roles into which they are forced, the colonized preserve a human identity and temporal being."[64] This is so, however, only to the extent that the silent resignation of the colonized is itself a form of passive resistance to colonial thingification. To be sure, the humanity of the colonized can be concretely reclaimed only in an explicit historico-political confrontation, since, as we shall see, the half-measure of resistance as silent resignation is itself prone to the temptation of dissolving and diluting the struggle in the imaginary world of arcane phantasmic myth.[65] Hidden under "the roles" forced on the colonized, one finds the smoldering tension of a subjugated and humiliated existence that needs to explode into open resistance if it is not to implode into an interior world of torpid and mystical self-mortification.

In what has been said thus far we have been expounding Fanon's views on violence in the colonial and the neocolonial situation. To be sure, all Fanon does is to articulate a prevalent theme of European philosophy in the context of Africa's experience of the modern Europeanized world. In other words: In Thomas Hobbes's conception of society, it is through the possibility of the uncompromising violence of the political state (i.e., the Leviathan) that order and stability are maintained.[66] In Hegel's famous dialectic of "lordship and bondage," it is through labor and in fear of death, the ultimate violence, and "the sovereign master" that the dialectic of "the master" and "the slave" unfolds. In Marx's idea of the class struggle it is through violent class conflict that the new is born out of the dying old society. In Heidegger's conception of the primordial *Polemos,* which is a violent "conflict that prevailed prior to everything divine and human," it is this primeval violence—as in Hesiod's *Theogony*—that "first projects and develops what had hitherto been unheard of, unsaid and un-thought."[67]

In differing ways, what is being articulated is a conception of violence which is fundamental to the varied problematics of the above thinkers and thus to the socio-political thinking of European philosophy. In this respect, it could be said that the whole contractarian perspective of modern political philosophy is grounded on a prolonged discourse on how to avert as well as to use violence for socially beneficial ends. Rousseau opens *The Social Contract* with a discussion of how force does not, of itself, have moral sanction. Hobbes, on the other hand, in the *Leviathan,* overcomes civil strife by instituting the state as the ultimate guarantor and embodiment of legitimate violence.

In talking about violence as he does, Fanon's novelty lies in the fact that his problematic is the concrete question of colonialism. Fanon describes the violence of colonial confrontation and in so doing shows us how "what had hitherto been unheard of, unsaid and unthought"— namely, the freedom of the colonized people of Africa—could come to pass. In this, Fanon does nothing more than specify within the colonial context what Heidegger articulates as the "*apolis*"[68] of human existence in the context of ancient Greek history and tragedy. This is the first emergence, the inauguration of a new order or "beginning" which "is the strangest and mightiest."[69] It is the originative violence with which Hesoid begins the *Theogony*. It is the foundational opening or origin that first institutes human existence in society—the *polis* (or community).

In Hegelian terms, Fanon's meditation on violence is an attempt to situate the dialectic of "lordship and bondage" within the colonial context, while being true to the historicity of Africa's encounter of Europe. In the section of *Black Skin, White Masks* (1952), titled "The Negro and Recognition" (section B of chapter 7), Fanon explicitly makes this the object of his deliberations. In fact, as Taylor puts it, "Fanon draws from the Hegelian-Marxist tradition" but in so doing reinterprets this tradition "in terms of the concrete specificity of the colonial situation."[70] Indeed, as Jean-Paul Sartre has astutely observed, in all of this, Fanon "acts as the interpreter of the [violent colonial] situation, that's all."[71]

The above notwithstanding, Hannah Arendt—an erudite scholar of the Occidental tradition—criticizes Fanon for glorifying violence in and for itself. In fact, Fanon is for Arendt one of the few thinkers who "glorified violence for violence's sake."[72] Nothing could be further from the truth. What Fanon does is to accurately depict the situation of conflict in the colonial context. In fact, as Arendt has observed, in the context of inter-European conflicts, the generation which lived under Nazi occupation found its freedom and salvation in "the resistance"—the *organized counter-violence* with which Europe defended itself against the brutality of Hitler's Germany.

In the midst of unsparing conflict, open and hidden, one does not philosophize. Violence understands only the language of violence. In Arendt's sagacious observation, the generation that lived the Nazi occupation found its "treasure" in violent confrontation. But what was this "treasure"?

As they themselves understood it, it seems to have consisted, as it were, of two interconnected parts: they had discovered that he who "joined the resistance, found himself," that he ceased to be "in quest of [himself] without mastery, in naked unsatisfaction," that he no longer suspected himself of "insincerity" of being "a carping, suspicious actor of life," that he could afford "to go naked." In this nakedness, stripped of all masks—of those which society assigns to its members as well as those which the individual fabricates for himself in his psychological reactions against society—they had been visited for the first time in their lives by *an apparition of freedom,* not, to be sure, because they acted against tyranny and things worse than tyranny—this was true for every soldier in the allied armies— but because they had become "*challengers,*" had taken the initiative upon themselves and therefore, without knowing or even noticing it, had begun to create that public space between themselves where *freedom could appear.*[73]

It is important to note that the character of Arendt's observation is impeccable. Those who fought the occupation found freedom. In confronting domination, they created and held open the "public space" in which "freedom could appear," not because they fought an odious tyranny, or because "they acted," but because "they took the initiative upon themselves" and in so doing became "challengers." In other words, it is the character of their actions that counts.

In joining the resistance one "found himself" precisely because one renounced passive submission to subjugation and engaged life. Those in the resistance made history by concretely reclaiming themselves, in the act of resisting, as human beings and thus "freedom could appear." Arendt understands all too well the existential import of *organized counter-violence* in the context of oppression and domination. Yet, what she recognizes in the European she fails to see in the non-European. The fact that Arendt does not see this can, at best, be attributed to her lack of sympathy for or understanding of colonized non-European peoples, or at worst, it could be taken as the symptom of a latent Eurocentric double standard at work in her thought.[74]

The colonized non-European, just like the generation of Europeans who lived under Nazi occupation, finds freedom and liberation in the resolved confrontation with the colonial apparatus. The colonized, in so doing, takes the initiative and carves out the "space" in which freedom can appear, thus overcoming colonial thingification. But why is this the case? It is precisely because colonialism—just as the Nazi occupation in respect to non-Aryans—is the complete negation of the historicity of the colonized. The very fact of conquest is taken by the colonizer as a metaphysical proof of the unhistoricity (i.e., the nonhumanness) of the colonized.

Colonialism is the blatant denial of the humanity of the colonized which serves as its own proof. It is the affirmation that the colonized have no history and are introduced into the human community by European conquest.[75] It is the violent claim that the colonized stand on the other side of the *difference* that constitutes humanity as human. Only by unleashing a self-redeeming counterclaim—and given the reality of colonialism and neocolonialism this can only be a counter-violence—can the colonized establish categorically to himself and to the colonizer the fact of his humanity.[76] As Fanon astutely points out in *A Dying Colonialism:*

> Before the rebellion there was the life, the movement, the existence of the settler, and on the other side the continued agony of the colonized. Since 1954 [the inception of the Algerian Revolution], the European has discovered that another life parallel to his own has *begun to stir,* and that is Algerian society.[77]

In this respect it has to be emphasized that the colonized does not choose violence. Violence is not a choice. It is the condition of existence imposed on the colonized by the colonizer, which enforces the colonized's status of being a "native," a *thing,* a historical being forcefully barred from history. In other words, the direct confrontation between the colonizer and the colonized is not the beginning of violence in the colonial situation. The "continued agony of the colonized" is in fact the historically grounding violence of colonialism.

In view of the above, any attempt to avert the violent conflict between the antagonists of colonial society—the moment the colonized begin to "stir"—is suspect, on the political level, for it is concretely implicated in the defense of colonialism. The feared "blood bath" will not commence with the awakening of the colonized. This hemorrhage is of long standing. This profuse loss of vitality, on the part of the colonized, is as old as the colonial settlement itself. This is what Albert Camus, an Algerian-born French citizen, fails to understand in all of his comments on the Algerian resistance in *Resistance, Rebellion and Death* (1960).[78] In like manner, all those who talk about violence in South Africa should ask themselves which violence they mean: that of the colonizer or of the colonized?

The counter-violence of the colonized is a *de-thingifying,* life-enhancing project of human liberation. The settler, a European migrant, originates in the systematic violence of colonization and expansion. The colony and the settler are the exteriorization of the dialectic of violence (i.e., poverty) internal to European modernity. As Memmi tells us, writing in 1957: "Today, the economic motives of colonial undertakings are revealed by every historian of colonialism."[79] The settler, in order to avoid the violence of poverty in Europe, where he is the victim of the socio-economic dialectic of modern European society, migrates to a foreign land and by force and violence makes others victims. The sheer egoism and inhumanity of this position is astounding. The more so because, as we noted earlier, the colonizer is duped by his own myths to such a point that he sees himself as the benefactor of those he victimizes.

In observing the settler's inhuman conduct and demeanor, the colonized learns that he can recover his freedom only by unleashing a counter-violence of his own. As Cabral emphatically and categorically points out,

> We are not defending the armed fight. . . . It is a violence against even our own people. But it is not our invention—it is not our cool decision; it is the *requirement of history*.[80]

For the colonized, violence is the avenue through which freedom and humanity are reclaimed. Violence is the "requirement of history" precisely because through it the colonized reclaims the possibility of human existence. This violence, furthermore, in being life-enhancing is also a violence that affects and fundamentally uproots the colonized.

The continual risking of life, the perpetual tension of confrontation against an odious enemy, the anxiety and intensity of a prolonged war, in short, the discipline and regimen of conflict purge the colonized of servility, dependence, cowardice, and similar vices that constitute the stunted existence of the colonized under colonialist conditions. In other words, the colonized

> formerly . . . a prey to unspeakable terrors yet happy to lose themselves in a dreamlike torment, such a people becomes unhinged, reorganizes itself, and in blood and tears gives birth to very real and immediate action.[81]

It is important to grasp the organic poise and poetry of Fanon's words. Just as a new being comes forth out of its mother's womb in "blood and tears" thus terminating the abnormal state of pregnancy, in like manner, the colonized in "blood and tears gives birth to" itself out of the lived historicity of the liberation struggle. The "very real and immediate action" of the struggle is thus the reverse of the static passivity of colonized existence. The colonizer makes history or historicizes by subjugating the "native" and replicating European society in a distorted manner.[82] The colonized, on the other hand, historicizes or enters the realm of human historical becoming in the determined confrontation with the colonial apparatus.

Colonialism literally freezes the internal dynamic of the subjugated society. In this situation, and in a futile attempt to diminish their wretchedness, the colonized produce out of their stagnant existence a fantastic magical world of sorcery and witchcraft. This is a realm of phantasms inhabited by "the dead who rise again, and the djinns who rush into your body while you yawn."[83] The ferocious unreality of this fantastic world is the ineffectual attempt by the colonized to displace—in the realm of the imaginary—the effective violence and terror of colonialism. This stunted "creativity," produced out of the native's lifeless and antiquated past, inadvertently adds to the stagnant and enigmatic reality of colonized "existence."

A noncolonized society grows, transforms, and, in all of this, constantly evaluates and re-evaluates its past in light of the future exigencies of its existence. As Nietzsche and Heidegger tell us, it is only in view of a future that a past is fruitfully appropriated. Colonized society, on the other hand, is not free to evaluate its past in terms of a possible future. It is a society without a future precisely because this is what colonialism negates and grounds itself on.

The violent confrontation with the colonial apparatus is the process through which this stagnant situation is eradicated. As Fanon puts it,

> the youth of a colonized country, growing up in an atmosphere of shot and fire . . . does not hesitate to pour scorn upon the zombies of his ancestors.[84]

In *A Dying Colonialism* (1959), taking the Algerian Revolution as his example, Fanon discusses in great detail how the struggle is a concrete process of historical self-creation. He does so in terms of the traditional attire (i.e., the veil), the relation of modern technology and medicine to the indigenous society, and the structure of subordination in the Algerian family. In all of this, Fanon shows how the struggle has a revitalizing and dynamic effect that puts into question the inert and superfluous dregs of the indigenous culture.

In confronting colonialism, the colonized projects a future and claims, for the vitality of the present, the effective heritage of the past. What he "jects" or throws ahead, in this emancipatory project, is his own effective and enduring heritage. This is what Aimé Césaire celebrates in his play *The Tragedy of King Christophe,* when he has his tragic hero say,

> Freedom yes, but not an easy freedom. Which means that they need a state. Yes, my philosopher friend, something that will enable this transplanted people to strike roots, to burgeon and flower, to fling the fruits and perfumes of its flowering into the face of the world, something which, to speak plainly, will oblige our people, by force if need be, to be born to itself, to surpass itself.[85]

The freedom Césaire advocates is a freedom which is constituted by the colonized's rebirth to "itself" in the fullness of its humanity. But why must the colonized "surpass itself"? Precisely because it does not suffice merely to expel the colonizer in order to effectively decolonize. It is further necessary to destroy the parasitic and ossified inert and residual Being-in-the-world of the colonized and to institute "the practices of freedom"[86] within the cultural and historical context of the decolonizing society, in the process of self-formation.

In decolonizing, the decolonized has to open up and claim its historical existence, its Being as history, closed off by colonial conquest. In so doing it reestablishes its political actuality in appropriating and living/practicing its existence in freedom. As Césaire's tragic hero, Christophe, forcefully asserts:

> This people's enemy is its indolence, its effrontery, its hatred of discipline, its self-indulgence, its lethargy. Gentlemen, for the honor and survival of this nation, I don't want it ever to be said, I won't have the world so much as suspect, that ten years of black freedom, ten years of black slovenliness and indifference, have sufficed to squander the patrimony that our martyred people has amassed in a hundred years of labor under the whip. You may as well get it through your heads this minute that with me you won't have the right to be tired.[87]

For Césaire what has to be reclaimed is not the "whip" or the multitude of social vices bred by slavery and unfreedom, but the "patrimony . . .

amassed in a hundred years of labor." The "patrimony" of endurance, fortitude, resistance, and creativity which, as Hegel tells us, constitutes the existential character of the slave in the dialectic of surmounting the master. This is the slave whose life experience is tempered by the immanent and ever-present possibility of death and the transfiguring creativity of productive labor. For Césaire "black freedom" is the effort of transcending enslavement aimed at instituting the historicity of the decolonized as decolonized.

Thus the violence of the colonized is also self-directed against the petrified forms of existence, whose actuality was the stagnant situation of external domination. In the struggle, the dying forms of existence in which the native found recourse and was forced to live as a "native" are thus challenged and *possibly* overcome. What concerns us here is the actualization, or failure thereof, of a definite historic *possibility*. Of course, in a very real way, if this does not happen—as Fanon tells us and as is concretely evinced by the actuality of neocolonial Africa—then:

> There's nothing save a minimum of readaptation, a few reforms at the top, a flag waving: and down there at the bottom an undivided mass, still living in the middle ages, endlessly marking time.[88]

As we noted in the beginning of this section, this is the stagnant actuality of neocolonialism. It is nothing more than the *de facto* renegotiation of the colonial status. That is why, as we noted earlier, all that is said of colonialism also holds true, in every essential, of neocolonial Africa.

Thus far, relying on Fanon, we have described the dialectic of violence and counter-violence that constituted, until very recently, colonial Africa and, by extension, constitutes our neocolonial present. Let us now briefly look at each aspect of the colonial and neocolonial situation.

III

The society of the settler is a cohesive and homogeneous community. The class distinctions internal to it are maintained, but in a friendly manner. The worker, the priest, the merchant are first and foremost settlers and only secondly members of this or that class or profession. The cohesiveness of the settler community is maintained against and in reference to the colonized, whose existence is fixed and frozen as the permanent underclass of this setup. The colony is the settler's own lived self-image. He foregrounds his individuality against the background of this collective. It is his domain, that in which his will and Being are embodied: the land that gave him his social and economic stability, the status he lacked in Europe.[89]

For the settler the colony is his salvation. He is, nonetheless, always a Frenchman or an Englishman in Algeria or Kenya, never an Algerian or a Kenyan. The settler cannot indigenize and remain a settler. His existence is innately parasitic. He is dependent on the mother country for his spiritual and historic legitimacy as a colonizer, and on the colony for his socio-economic existence and preeminence. The duplicity of this situation, as noted earlier, is the grounding source of colonial fascism.[90]

On the other hand, the colonized's existence is not cohesive but split in two. Within the colonized part of the colonial structure we have the *urban* and the *rural* native: in other words, those who have been Westernized and who, as Fanon puts it, "profit—at a discount, to be sure—from the colonial setup"[91] and the rural peasant/nomad masses who experience colonialism only or mostly as an external control and imposition.

At this point, it is important to note that this split is the originative ground of neocolonialism. In creating and maintaining this fracture among the colonized, colonial conquest establishes the material and cultural conditions in which the self-aggrandizing metaphysical delusions of Europe can be institutionally established, by being embodied in the consciousness and the physical actuality of "independent" Africa.[92]

The actuality of conquest confirms, after the fact, the servility of the colonized. Subjugation is thus historicized into and as the historicity of African existence.[93] This requires and presupposes the cultural negation of Westernized (i.e., modernized) Africans, whose very existence, as a section of the colonized society, was predicated on the rupture of African existence in the face of European conquest. Non-Europeanized Africa, on the other hand, was forced to submit to a stagnant petrification of its cultural, economic, historical, and political actuality. The peoples of the continent—in all the wealth of their diverse traditions— were thus reduced to a frozen existence as a subaltern and passive element in the historical eventuation of European modernity. As we saw in chapter 2, under the guise of the African's oneness with nature, it is this subordinate passivity of African existence under European dominance that Senghor celebrates as *Africanité*.[94]

Thus the inheritance and actuality of post-colonial Africa manifests itself and is basically grounded on the schizoid existence of two complementary and yet violently contradictory modes of African (non)-Being-in-the-world: the Westernized dominating and the indigenous dominated native. Encased between these two forms of estranged existence one finds the presence of the present. These two paradoxical types replicate and constantly reproduce by proxy the colonizing historical-ness of Europe and the historical stasis of present-day Africa. It is from within this situation, as we saw in the preceding chapter, that Nkrumah and Hountondji advocate an abstract and "universalistic" Marxism-Leninism instead of concretely submitting this stagnant situation to scrutiny.[95]

As graphically depicted by Sembene Ousmane in his 1968 film *Mandabi,* it is the estranging dialectic of these two broad segments of society that constitutes the contemporary crisis of the continent.[96] These two segments of African society parrot the estranged and estranging violent dialectic of the colonizer and the colonized, described so well by Memmi. But, in this case, the roles of colonizer and colonized are played by the native, cast on both sides of this antagonistic and complementary divide by reference to the culture and "know-how" (i.e., political and economic managerial skills, technology, science, etc.) of the former colonial power.[97] The Westernized African, in this context, is "Caliban become Prospero."[98]

Insofar as the anti-colonial struggle is aimed at overcoming colonialism and neocolonialism, it is an attempt to end the fissure in African existence between Westernized dominating and indigenous dominated Africa. It is in overcoming this split and in the positive union or fusion of these two broad segments of African society that the counter-violence of the colonized acquires a political form and becomes a project for a possible future of freedom. In fact, demographically and sociologically speaking, African liberation movements are born out of the "fusion of horizons" of these two broad segments of African society.[99]

Each manifests, in itself, what the other does not have and is estranged from. The Westernized native is acquainted with the world beyond the colony or neocolony and the struggles of other peoples. The rural non-Westernized native, on the other hand, is steeped in the broken heritage of his own particular African past. In the fusion of these two fractured "worlds" the possibility of African freedom is concretized or made tangible in the form of specific historical movements.

The struggle is a historically pedagogical and a concretely self-formative process. Its success is measured by the extent to which it overcomes the "Manichean world"[100] of colonialism and neocolonialism. In other words, "the settler is not simply the man who must be killed" and "not every Negro or Moslem is issued automatically a hallmark of genuineness." The struggle is successful to the extent that it breaks down the "barriers of blood and race-prejudice . . . on both sides."[101] Unthinking prejudices are thus displaced by the prejudgments cultivated out of the lived experience of the struggle. It is thus that "the practices of freedom" are established in the context of the African liberation struggle.

In like manner, in a neocolonial context, it is when the Westernized native puts "at the people's disposal the intellectual and technical capital that it has snatched when going through the colonial universities"[102] that the dialectic of violence and counter-violence is sublated in the reconstitution of a new ethical whole, of a new *ethos*. This is the process, as we saw in chapter 1, that appropriates the possibilities of a specific tradition from within the lived confines and concrete possibilities of that tradition itself.[103]

Tempered by and produced out of the lived exigencies of the struggle, and grounded on the concrete experiencing—with all its limitations and creative possibilities—of its own mortal existence, a very practical and pragmatic rationality dominates and directs the development of this *praxis* of concrete communal self-creation. This is the lived quotidian self-formative *ethos* of the liberation struggle—"the practices of freedom." It is what Marx refers to as the dialectical process through which the educators are themselves educated.[104]

In view of all of the above then, and beyond the initial moment of counter-violence, the African liberation struggle is an originative process through which the historicity of the colonized is reclaimed and appropriated anew. In chapter 4 we shall see how this process is grasped and formulated in the thinking of Fanon and Cabral. As we shall see, in their situated thinking, African philosophical hermeneutics finds its most eminent forerunners and paradigmatic exemplars.

Thus, in contradistinction to Senghor and Ethnophilosophy, on the one hand, and Nkrumah, Hountondji, and Professional Philosophy, on the other, this will be our hermeneutical response to the question: What are the people of Africa trying to free themselves from and what are they trying to establish?

4

The Liberation Struggle
Existence and Historicity

"Exactly," exclaimed Djia Umrel. "What model of society are we offered through the media? We're made to swallow outdated values, no longer accepted in their countries of origin. Our television and radio programmes are stupid. And our leaders, instead of foreseeing and planning for the future, evade their duty. Russia, America, Europe, and Asia are no longer examples or models for us."

"It would be a dangerous step backwards, to revert to our traditions. . . ."

"That's not what I'm saying, Joom Galle," she interrupted. "We must achieve a synthesis. . . . Yes, a synthesis. . . . I don't mean a step backwards. . . . A new type of society," she ended, blinking. There followed a brief silence.

—Sembene Ousmane
From *The Last of the Empire*, 1981

In an interview given in 1984 the French thinker Michel Foucault, in characterizing the focus of his thought, refers to liberty and liberation as being constituted by the self-formative "practice of the self"[1] on the self. The interviewer asks: "A work of self upon self which can be understood as a kind of liberation, as a mode of liberation?" To which Foucault responds, in part:

> I shall be a little more cautious about that. I've always been a little distrustful of the general theme of liberation, to the extent, that . . .

[it refers] back to the idea that there does exist a nature or a human foundation which, as a result of a certain number of historical, social or economic processes, found itself concealed, alienated or imprisoned in and by some repressive mechanism. In that hypothesis it would suffice to unloosen these repressive locks so that man can be reconciled with himself. . . . I don't think that [this] is a theme which can be admitted without rigorous examination. I do not mean to say that liberation or such and such a form of liberation does not exist. When a colonial people tries to free itself of its colonizer, that is truly an act of liberation, in the strict sense of the word. But as we also know, that in this extremely precise example, this act of liberation is *not sufficient* to establish the *practices of liberty* that later on will be necessary for this people, this society and these individuals to decide upon receivable and *acceptable forms of their existence or political society.* That is why I insist on *the practice of freedom.*[2]

I have quoted extensively from Foucault precisely because he puts his finger on the central theme of this chapter: the question of the "forms of existence or political society" that can vindicate and properly fulfill the aspirations of the African struggle against colonialism and neocolonialism.

To the interviewer's blunt question Foucault responds with a conditional: If liberation means a return to an original "nature" or "human foundation," then such a theoretic project, on metaphysical and epistemic grounds, is untenable. On the other hand, anti-colonial struggles are "truly an act of liberation" that need to establish "the practice of freedom" in order to realize their own emancipatory goals. As Foucault pointedly observes, "the struggle for liberation is indispensable for the practice of liberty"[3] but it is not enough. On this point, given the central problematic of this study as a whole, the question is: How does one establish the practice or *ethos* of freedom in the process of liberating one's existence from external—direct or indirect—domination?

The "practice of freedom" or liberty is grounded on and arises out of the self-formative *ethos* of a people—the temporality or the way of Being of a people. In our context this occurs in the concrete process of struggle of differing African peoples to actualize their free existence. This presupposes the liberation struggle as it unfolds within the context of specific and particular histories, and with it the *concrete implementation*—the practice—of liberty which is the formal and proclaimed *raison d'être* of the struggle in its very inception.

The term *ethos*, as Foucault reminds us alluding to the Greeks, refers to "the deportment"[4] of a people in its public politico-ethical existence. Thus, beyond the violence and counter-violence of colonialism and neocolonialism (i.e., the subject matter of chapter 3), Foucault is interested in the possibility and the practical actuality of freedom. In appropriating Foucault's astute remarks my concern is to see how this self-formative *ethos* (i.e., "the practice of freedom") has manifested itself, or failed to do so, thus far in the historic eventuations of the African liberation struggle.

Reflecting on this question in the last chapter of his book, *Africa in Modern History*, the eminent Africanist historian Basil Davidson notes that the African countries that achieved independence in the late 1950s and early 1960s were wedded to colonial attitudes and values. Thus: "Old inequalities from the pre-colonial heritage, whether between man and man or more plainly between man and woman, were enlarged by new inequalities from the colonial heritage," and to this extent the regimes of the late 1950s and early 1960s were "the oppressors and exploiters of the many by the few" in African guise.[5] This neocolonial "independence" was a *de facto* extension of colonialism—the violent negation, at the very moment of its possible attainment, of the "practice of freedom."

In contradistinction to the above, starting from the early 1970s an indigenous and much more radically democratic conception of liberation took root in various African liberation struggles. This perspective did not originate *de novo*, but commenced by critically differentiating itself from the kind of "independence" established in the late 1950s and early 1960s. The critical standard or gauge of this rejection was grounded on the failure of "independent" Africa to concretely live up to and appropriate/actualize its formal status of independence.

From the outset, it is important to note that this critical orientation was not an abstract quest for utopia, but a radical "revolutionary undertaking . . . directed not only against the present but against the rule of 'until now.' "[6] In concrete and practical terms, this critique was grounded on the contrast between the miserable situation of post-colonial Africa and the purely formal and empty status of political "independence." It was grounded on the lived and stark contrast between unfulfilled *ideals* and harsh unforgiving political *realities*. This immanent and critical orientation was thus directed internally toward its own lived historical situatedness. In countering itself to the despotic politics of post-colonial "independent" Africa, this trend established the practice of participatory popular democracy as the cornerstone and gauge of its own political existence. In so doing, in differing ways and out of the lived exigencies of differing African histories and specific contexts, it articulated a notion of liberation as a process of reclaiming history.

In Hegelian terms, one could say that in countering itself to the established neocolonialist order, this critique saw itself as the political articulation and concrete historical incarnation of the negativity of the negative in contemporary African political life. In Hegel's *Phenomenology of Spirit* the odyssey of consciousness (i.e., the differing forms through which *Geist* manifests itself in history) realizes itself by overcoming itself through and by the mediation of the negative. In like manner, this critical orientation of the early 1970s saw itself as the initial moment in the process of reclaiming the historicity of existence and concretely actualizing the unfulfilled aspirations of African independence. It saw itself as the negativity of the negative in the process of self-overcoming.

In discussing this radical and fundamental orientation, Davidson specifically points to the theoretic perspective articulated by Amilcar Cabral and his comrades in the PAIGC (*Partido Africano da Independencia da Guine e Cabo Verde*).[7] Thus, in view of what has been said up to this point, my basic concern in this chapter is to see how this popular and democratic trend establishes "the practice of freedom" in the context of implementing its conception of African liberation as a process of reclaiming history.

I will begin with Fanon, to thematically locate the political context of this process. Consequent on the above, Cabral's formulation of liberation as a "return to the source" will be given as a specific example of reclaiming the historicity of African existence. This process, unleashed by African societies and individuals in liberating themselves, is the act of historically instituting "receivable and acceptable forms of existence or political society" in the context of differing histories. For ultimately—when all is said and done and beyond race and color— the actuality of these differing histories constitutes our lived humanity as Africans.

Let us now, with Fanon, begin by examining this process on the continental level of Africa, which we will then concretize by examining the specific theoretic formulations of Cabral in the context of Guinea-Bissau. In this, my intention is not to give an exhaustive sociological and historical analysis of Cabral's thought.[8] My only concern is to give a concrete and practical depiction of reclaiming history as a specific instance of "the practice of freedom."

I

Following on his detailed examination of the violence and counter-violence endemic to colonialism in *The Wretched of the Earth*, Fanon poses the cardinal question as to how this situation of violence is to be overcome beneficially for the colonized.

> What are the forces which in the colonial period open up new outlets and engender new aims for *the violence of the colonized peoples*? In the first place there are the *political parties*.[9]

To be sure, the question Fanon poses is the question of the urban (i.e., Westernized) and rural native. In the concluding pages of the previous chapter we preliminarily noted that it is in the fusion of these two differing horizons that the possibility of African freedom is established. We need now to look at the political context and the elemental dynamic within and out of which this historically originative fusion takes place. Thus, with Fanon and in keeping with Cornelius Castoriadis's pioneering work, *The Imaginary Institution of Society*, we will examine the grounding process of the concrete self-institution of society (the reclaiming of history) in the context of the African situation.[10]

As Fanon insightfully observes, in the urban nationalist "political parties" we find at work a paradoxical African political consciousness. In other words, in the "nationalist parties" we find linked together "the will to break colonialism" and "another quite different will: that of coming to a friendly agreement with it."[11] The political parties are in the first place of and for the urban center. They are political organizations whose point of reference is European political practice and theory. Their basic orientation is the politics of calculated mass unrest, manipulated toward the orderly displacement of power from one elite to another. Their basic objective is the transfer of power from Europeans to Africans (i.e., to themselves) in a methodic manner. Their only concern is to demonstrate that they can calm and stabilize the volatile situation of violence and chaos.

For these political parties the urgency of the popular unrest is located in its power to convince the colonizer of their necessity and importance. These parties cohabit and share the political space and discourse of colonialism. They are above all else "reasonable" since they are susceptible to the rationality of the colonizer. As Senghor, the paradigm of the Westernized native *par excellence*, points out, when "examined more profoundly, on the level of universal history"[12] colonialism has both a debit and a credit side. In this respect "we, the colonized of yesterday . . . shall be more attentive to contributions than to defects."[13] It is of cardinal importance to note here that "we" refers to Westernized Africans—those who can appreciate the positive value of "universal history" as unfolded thus far in the colonialist historicity of Europe, since, as Fanon sarcastically and pointedly observes, for "[t]he 'jungle savage' . . . certain factors have not yet acquired importance."[14]

Indeed, these parties, composed of more or less Westernized natives that appreciate "on the level of universal history" the "contributions" of colonialism to the colonized, play a historically paradoxical role: On the one hand, they are the mediating link between colonialism and neocolonialism; and on the other, they abstractly formulate the concrete possibility of African freedom. They "abstractly" contemplate the "concrete" process and possibility of African self-emancipation.

The urban nationalist parties, modeled on European trade unions and emulating their political practice, cater to the needs of the Westernized native. They placate the political vanity of the *assimilado* caste/class, those who abhor local village and town politics (tribalism?), but avidly follow world events and conflicts—the *événements* in Paris and London. Shopkeepers, chauffeurs, clerks, self-proclaimed fashion/society ladies, minor experts, graduates of correspondence schools, Westernized intellectuals, in short, that segment of society called into existence by colonialism and "sprinkled" with European culture is politically serviced by these parties.

This is the section of indigenous society that on the whole, like Kafka's humanized ape, suspects its own indigenous culture and history of being worthless.[15] Its very existence, from its dating habits to its professional biases, is structured by a desperate and narcissistic attempt to mimic, duplicate, and *be* Europe in every respect.[16] This caste of people, within itself, is defined and differentiated in terms of the extent of extroversion and dependency of its constituent members. In all of this, Europe and European existence is the standard of excellence. Those who are culturally closest to Europe are thus also the leaders of the pack.

On the other hand, the political parties function in total disregard of the rural native and the "lumpenproletariat," the perpetually unemployed *displaced peasantry*, the coolie labor which inhabits the shanties surrounding the European urban centers of the periphery. When these parties concern themselves with the rural native, they do so as "generous benefactors" who have come to enlighten the backward residue of history. They " 'parachute' organizers into the villages" in order to "erect a framework around the people which follows an *a priori* schedule."[17] Needless to say, this "*a priori* schedule" is traced out of the political eventuations of European history which simultaneously falsify and estrange indigenous political life.

The urban parties are not inserted in the lived needs and concerns that move and define the life of the rural native. The interior of the colony or neocolony is seen as inhospitable territory in spite of the freedom slogans proclaimed by the urban parties. The politics of village affairs and local conflicts, "the only existing national events," are trampled under foot by the "makers of the future nation's history."[18] As Fanon pointedly observes, they do not "put their theoretical knowledge to the service of the people" but rather, they intend to *use* the rural mass and its hopes for their own rather narrow, avaricious, and self-indulgent political objectives.[19]

Simultaneously, and because they present themselves as the interpreters of the aspirations of freedom and use appropriate if abstract slogans for this purpose, these parties produce or attract to their ranks individuals concretely tuned in to the needs and emancipatory possibilities of the anti-colonial or anti-neocolonial struggle. In other words, these parties are hybrid formations called into existence by the process of the struggle, which as a rule transcends their narrow historical grasp of the historic moment in which they exist.

At this point, it is imperative to note that it is the volcanic and eruptive "violence of the colonized peoples" which produces these same parties as outlets and later on, in its maturation, surpasses and sheds them, much as a snake sheds its first skin. In fact and from the very outset, the concrete possibility for self-emancipation harbored by this process of struggle is both hidden and disclosed by these parties. These parties abstractly formulate slogans and platforms which, if historically realized, would lead to their own political demise. Thus, from their midst arise the implementers of this demise.

Obviously there are to be found at the core of the political parties and among their leaders certain revolutionaries who deliberately turn their backs upon the farce of national independence. But very quickly their questionings, their energy and their anger obstruct the party machine; and these elements are gradually isolated, and then quite simply brushed aside. At this moment, as if there existed a dialectic concomitance, the colonialist [or neocolonialist] police will fall upon them. With no security in the towns, avoided by the militants of their former party and rejected by its leaders, these undesirable firebrands will be stranded in county districts. Then it is that they will realize bewilderedly that the peasant [nomad] masses catch on to what they have to say immediately, and without delay ask them the question to which they have not yet prepared the answer: "When do we start?"[20]

It is in and out of this fusion of necessity that the urban and rural native *encounter* each other, *for the first time*, as possible co-protagonists in a process of political struggle and originative history. As Fanon notes in the sentence following the above quotation, the "meeting [or fusion] of revolutionaries coming from the towns [Westernized natives] and country dwellers [peasants/nomads]"[21] is the dynamic locus out of which unfolds the dialectic of African self-emancipation.

In being "stranded in the county districts" the Westernized urban "revolutionaries," for whom politics is both a calling and a passionate vocation, find the human actuality whose needs and situation their radical discourse has thus far only abstractly articulated. The "people," the "masses," become very concrete in this encounter, in all of their cultural complexity and material misery. For the peasants/nomads, the bulk of the rural mass and the majority of the country are the sector of the indigenous populace which is totally disregarded by the calculations of the urban parties. They are the ones who will suffer concretely (famine and perpetual administrative/political neglect) from the "farce of national independence." Thus, out of this encounter emerges a mutual recognition between the urban and rural native of what is at stake: colonialism minus the "whites," or the possibility of instituting freedom in the process of struggle.

It is only when certain elements from within the urban parties realize their folly in practice and are *forced* into a concrete collaboration with the rural native that the impasse of neocolonialism, incarnated in the urban parties, is possibly overcome. When out of practical-pragmatic political necessity certain groups and parties come to realize that the historicity of the struggle is directly tied to the concrete concerns of the rural mass, only then is a political practice of freedom truly possible. But how might this possibility be actualized?

It is imperative to note that this dialectic of freedom is ignited by historically contingent situations. In reaction to some specific problem, certain elements within a political party or a liberation front put in question the effectiveness of the methods used thus far. Or in some cases, a political party reexamines its stance in terms of the actuality and the needs of the interior regions of the country (for example: the radical reorientation of the PAIGC after the Pidgiguiti massacre of 1959).[22] In all of this it has to be emphasized that the concrete and historic situation itself becomes the standard and testing ground of the radical possibilities of the liberation struggle.

In this context, the questioning of these elements, usually the most dynamic and radical within the established parties, irritates and destabilizes the accepted norms of political discourse. In and out of this context these "dangerous" elements are forcefully marginalized.[23] These groups, self-exiled to the interior to avoid persecution, find a populace immersed in a totally different world. They discover that the peasants and nomads have their own politics (i.e., concerns for the protection of traditional rights, the improvement of social and economic conditions, etc.) for which they are ready and willing to sacrifice. In this encounter the former urban militants come to recognize that the politics of the "center" and the lived political actuality of the "periphery" are mutually exclusive and antithetical. Thus, in contrast to the "café politicians" the militant finds—in the "dark" interior, in the countryside—a receptive, eager, and enlightened audience.

It cannot be emphasized enough that this encounter between "militants with the police on their track and these mettlesome masses of people, who are rebels by instinct,"[24] *is not* the implementation of some theoretic formula or a voluntary/willed encounter. It is rather a specific junction—which does not and need not always and of necessity occur—in the unfolding of the liberation struggle. Furthermore, when it does occur, it need not occur in exactly the way described by Fanon. Its occurrence, however, is the *sine qua non* of the possibility of "the practice of freedom" in the context of the African liberation struggle. For it brings together the urban militants with those for whom

> militating in a national party is not simply taking part in politics; it is choosing the only means whereby they can pass from the status of an animal to that of a human being.[25]

Or, as Fanon even more graphically puts it in *Black Skin, White Masks*:

> For the Negro who works on a sugar plantation in Le Robert, there is only one solution: to fight. He will embark on this struggle, and he will pursue it, not as the result of a Marxist or idealistic analysis [i.e., not as a result of theory] but quite simply because he cannot

conceive of life otherwise than in the form of a battle against exploitation, misery, and hunger.[26]

In this *encounter* of the urban militant and the rural mass is made possible within the context of contemporary African history, the originative moment of the fundamental self-institution of human societies and histories.[27] This encounter or fusion is the coming together of the seething subterranean elemental forces that thus far had been checked and held in stasis by the established colonial or neocolonial order. It is only out of this eruptive and magmatic flow of historic possibilities that "the practice of freedom" can possibly be established.

The image/metaphor of "magma," which I borrow from Castoriadis, has to be envisaged as a volcanic eruption and the subsequent gush and solidification of molten rock. The fluidity of the magma hardens into differing forms that *invent themselves* as the lava flow slowly solidifies. Unlike Hegelian or Marxist conceptions of history, this metaphor gives us to understand the historicity of existence as completely fluid and grounded on the lived and "inherent plastic power" of those engaged in it.[28] The happening of history, understood in this manner, is the unreplicable process through which radically novel historical formations are self-invented and concretely self-instituted.[29] This eruptive historical self-creation always occurs in terms of concrete needs and in response to specific historic pressures and limit situations.

The occurrence, in whatever form, of this eruptive process of fusion is essential. As Fanon points out in the section of *The Wretched of the Earth* titled "The Pitfalls of National Consciousness," and as is evident in the contemporary politics of Africa (i.e., the defunct actuality of the Organization of African Unity) the non-occurrence of this eruptive fusion leads to the failure of the promise of African liberation—the contemporary actuality of neocolonialism. In other words: "There's nothing save a minimum of readaptation, a few reforms at the top, a flag waving: and down there at the bottom an undivided mass . . . endlessly marking time."[30]

In the name of freedom and independence the urban native in power—the African dependent bourgeoisie—becomes the agent of Euro-American (i.e., NATO) economic, political, and cultural dominance. Independence does not usher in the concrete vitalization of the indigenous populace or the institution of structures (political, economic, cultural, etc.) on a national level that enhance and confirm the freedom of the formerly colonized. Rather, the cities remain the centers of European mimicry and the interior is frozen, mummified, and held in stasis as the enclave of "ethnic cultures"—much valued and advertized by the newly established National Tourist Bureau. The political economy of Euro-American leisure (tourism?) is in fact one of the main preoccupations and source of revenue of neocolonial states.[31] Indeed, security (i.e., a police state existence for the vast majority of the local populace), wildlife preserves, and ethnic "cultural" exhibitions equal foreign exchange.

The policies that emanate from the "center" are geared toward the politics and economics of Europe, the original *center* of the colonial and now of the neocolonial setup. Cash crops and the export of raw materials are complemented by ethnic "parliamentary" procedures on ethnic "socialist" edicts directed by the single-party state,[32] the enclave of the urban native, which simultaneously uses the antiquated ethnic animosities of the rural native to good advantage. Even the old colonial policy of "divide and rule" remains intact, precisely because the transfer of power does

> not take place at the level of structures . . . since that caste [the Westernized African bourgeois] has done nothing more than take over unchanged the legacy of the economy, the thought, and the institutions left by the colonialists.[33]

Thus it happens that the former leaders of the movement (Senghor, Kenyatta, etc.) become the "transmission line" between the nation and its former colonizers. Development, nationalization of land and industry, and all the radical slogans of the movement (African Socialism?) become mere words in the politics of deception and intimidation. A single-party state is proclaimed and its leaders engage in systematically "expelling" those who fought for independence "from history or preventing them from taking root in it."[34]

Against this negative possibility, Fanon asserts that the rooting of the populace in history is the concrete regearing of the politics and economics of the newly independent state toward and in the interest of the rural populace. For the rooting of the masses in history is the magmatic flow through which the formerly colonized become active participants in their own historical existence or Being. This rooting in history is expressed in the decentralization of political power and the diversification of economic production, on all levels, aimed at empowering the common folk. Only when this becomes a lived actuality at the grass-roots level, through the establishment of local mass political institutions of peoples' power (peoples' assemblies, village associations, etc.) in which popular democracy is implemented, only in such a context is "the practice of freedom" possible. For this phrase, which I have borrowed from Foucault, means nothing more than the concrete and lived self-governance of the previously colonized or neocolonized populace.[35] As Fanon puts it: "The people must understand what is at stake. Public business ought to be the business of the public."[36] Only when and if this is achieved in an actual and meaningful way can one say that freedom and sovereignty, in a real sense, have been instituted in the life and *as the life* of common ordinary folk.

As already noted, in the context of armed conflict, it is in the process of securing the survival of the movement that the conditions for the possibility of "the practice of freedom" are originally created.[37] The openness of the rural and urban native each to the other, the eagerness of the common folk to fulfill the needs of the moment, is an imperative of existence both for the movement as a whole and for the individuals that compose it.

> The real people, the men and the women, the children and the old people in the colonized country [or the section of the populace in the liberated areas of a neocolony], take it for granted [if they are to survive!] that existing, in the biological sense of the word, and existing as a sovereign people are synonymous. The only possible issue, the sole way of salvation for this people is to react as energetically as it can to the genocide campaign being conducted against it.[38]

In this context, politics, or "the struggle," and everyday life are not two things apart. It is the effective development of the struggle which establishes the possibility of quotidian existence. But this effective development is itself possible only if it evokes the concerned and voluntary involvement and participation of the indigenous populace. This commitment in turn is assured only if the organized movement seriously engages the needs of the rural mass and is actively recognized as doing so. The struggle, in short, secures the support of the mass to the extent that it concretely involves the common folk on all levels, and in doing so helps them metamorphose themselves from inert ahistorical beings absent from history into active and jealous protagonists of their own historical becoming existence.

In this inter-implicative dialectic between armed groups and their popular mass base, daily life is not defined by its indifference to politics/history but becomes that which makes for its possibility.[39] In this context, the urban militants stranded in the interior have to learn to "make do" with the mass among whom they find themselves. Political engagement loses its abstract replicability (Marxist-Leninist formulas?) and becomes the constant attempt to be relevant to lived experience. The abstract slogans of "café politics" have to be concretized or discarded. The needs of the struggle act as a sieve and the multi-leveled combat becomes the filtering process, the avenue through which the urban militant finds his way back to the historicity of the indigenous mass.

If he is a teacher (Lumumba), a mechanic, an engineer, a doctor (Fanon), or an agronomist (Cabral) by profession, he puts his skills to work and adjusts them to the situation. In so doing he learns and becomes tuned to the concerns and needs of the rural mass, recognizing thus that to be politically engaged means confronting these concrete needs (not quoting Mao!) within the context of the present. In this lived involvement, the former urban militant becomes a "*Maquisard*"—a freedom fighter. This is how Fanon puts it:

> Since they are obliged to move about the whole time in order to escape from the police . . . they will have good reason to wander through their country and to get to know it. The cafes are forgotten; so are the arguments. . . . Their ears hear the true voice of the country, and their eyes take in the great and infinite poverty of their people. They realize the precious time that has been wasted in useless commentaries. . . . The men coming from the towns learn their lessons in the hard school of the people, and at the same time these men open classes for the people in military and political education. The people furnish up their weapons; but in fact the classes do not last long, for the masses come to know once again the strength of their own muscles, and push the leaders to prompt action.[40]

It cannot be emphasized enough that this process of fusion does not happen as a result of official and formal proclamations or affirmations. It occurs out of *cohabiting* the same historical, political, and existential space in the midst of the most concrete and ultimate of human possibilities—death. It occurs by osmosis and diffusion—the way an exile assimilates the mannerisms and language of his hosts.

Just as the urban militant is cultured into the values and concerns of the rural native, conversely, in this context, the peasants/nomads reclaim their human existence and cultural heritage not as a frozen relic of a dead past, but as the living culture of an actuality—historical and political—in the process of self-institution. As we noted in chapter 3, in *L'An Cinq de la Révolution Algérienne*, Fanon gives us a detailed account of this process of historical revival. He concretely documents for us Castoriadis's metaphor of magmatic gush, flow, and solidification as he lived and experienced it in the first five years of the Algerian anti-colonial struggle.[41] It is in this concrete sense then that, for Fanon, the struggle at a fundamental level necessitates the radical metamorphosis of traditional society.[42] It is in this context that contemporary concerns are appropriated into the lived actuality of the liberation movement.

From this point on, ancient/ossified customs and traditions are not merely discarded out of hand by the urban native, nor are they desperately held on to by the rural native. Rather, their preservation loses its inertia and becomes a process by which society is historically reinstituted out of the needs of the present mediated by the struggle. The future is here not the inert and continued perpetuation of colonial dominance; rather it is the projection of the possibilities embedded in the fusion of the rural and urban native. In this process the arrested heritage of native society is vitalized in discarding and appropriating that which is necessary for its survival.

Borrowing a phrase from Hans-Georg Gadamer, the struggle as embodied in the encounter of the urban and rural native can be described as a "fusion of horizons"[43] arising from the concrete historicity of the colonized in the process of self-emancipation. For Gadamer, the lived consciousness which is saturated with history—in our context, the consciousness incarnated in the historicalness of the liberation movement—is open and predisposed to the possibilities of its own historicity. Thus, in this *encounter* of the urban and rural native, the standpoint of the present is put in question and what is appropriated is not the inert past but the effective historicity of the fusion of these two elemental and dynamic forces. This is what Gadamer refers to as the "effective-historical consciousness," concretely grasped within the context of the African situation.[44]

It is in this sense that Fanon's references to history and to reinstituting the history of the former colonized has to be understood. In this regard Fanon writes:

> The setting up of the colonial system does not of itself bring about the death of the native culture. Historic observation reveals, on the contrary, that the aim sought is rather a continued agony than a total disappearance of the pre-existing culture. This culture, once living and open to the future, becomes closed, fixed in the colonial status, caught in the yoke of oppression. Both present and mummi-

> fied, it testifies against its members. It defines them without appeal.
> The cultural mummification leads to a mummification of individual
> thinking. The apathy so universally noted among colonial peoples
> is but the logical consequence of this operation.[45]

Colonialism petrifies the subjugated culture. It becomes estrangement
and abnegation (tribalism?) for the Westernized native. On the other
hand, it prescribes for the rural native an inert existence whose present
is an irrelevant past. This is the state of affairs that needs to be
overcome.

If decolonization is truly to be what it claims to actualize—the
"advent of peoples . . . onto the stage of history"[46]—then it has to
become a *truly* lived historical and political actuality. To be sure, this
is not an argument for cultural autarchy. It does not mean reinstituting
a *dead* but an "authentic" African past, "living it as a defence mechanism, as a symbol of purity, of salvation." It does not refer to a "culture
put into capsules, which has vegetated since the foreign domination."[47]

In all that has been said thus far, for Fanon, the liberation struggle
overcomes the "Pitfalls of National Consciousness" only when that
which was affirmed *de facto* in the process of the struggle—the eruptive
fusion of the urban and rural native—is concretely instituted *de jure*
as the lived actuality of the independent state.

> The struggle for freedom does not give back to the national culture its
> former value and shape; this struggle which aims at a *fundamentally
> different set of relations between men* [i.e., "the practice of free-
> dom"] cannot leave intact either the form or the content of the
> people's culture. After the conflict there is not only the disappearance
> of colonialism but also the disappearance of the colonized man.[48]

These are inspired and hopeful words! Indeed, those of us of the present
are painfully aware of the fact that the demise of colonialism has not,
as of yet, resulted in the "disappearance of the colonized man." Most
of Africa today suffers neocolonialism under the rule of such "men."
This historical observation, however, does not in any way detract an
iota from the veracity of the position articulated by Fanon. It says
nothing, in principle, against the future prospects of this position. It
only indicates that, to date, the African liberation struggle has failed
in its promise—articulated in a multitude of documents and programs—to reclaim the historicity of African existence.

Guarantees are, of course, out of the question in things human and historical. The above notwithstanding, however, in the theoretic perspective of Cabral we see the viability of Fanon's hopes articulated from within the concrete context of Guinea-Bissau. Let us now turn to Cabral for, as Fanon tells us, beyond abstract affirmations the African liberation struggle is the lived experience of specific national movements.[49]

II

It is necessary to note at this point that the process of reclaiming history which I have been describing thus far in the thinking of Fanon was the actual lived experience of the generation of Westernized Africans who fought and participated in the defeat of Portuguese colonialism—the first and last European empire in Africa. As Cabral puts it:

> I remember very well how some of us still students, got together in Lisbon, influenced by the currents which were shaking the world, and began to discuss one day what could today be called the re-Africanization of our minds.[50]

These discussions led Cabral and other *assimilados* of his generation back to Africa to reorient themselves and reclaim their African heritage.

Prior to becoming one of the key figures in the founding of the *Partido Africano da Independencia da Guine e Cabo Verde* (PAIGC), the movement that defeated Portuguese colonialism in Guinea-Bissau, Cabral worked for a number of years as an agronomist for the Portuguese and in this capacity studied the soil while absorbing the differing cultures of his native land.[51] It is this lived experience of "re-Africanisation" which Cabral systematically develops into the conception of revolution—in the African context—as a "return to the source."[52] Let us now closely follow and probe Cabral's thinking on this point.

The basic premise of Cabral's thinking on colonialism and the anti-colonial struggle, which he formulates as the "return to the source," is a heteronomous and multivalent conception of history. For Cabral as for Heidegger, "existence is revealed in many ways."[53] History or culture is the actuality of engagements, intellectual (artistic/spiritual) and material, in which a people unveils its existence. In commerce with their natural environment and in the context of definite social relations and an inherited past, differing histories and cultures are formed. Differing peoples always exist within the confines of specific histories/cultures that disclose and are disclosed by the lived actuality of a people.

For Cabral history/culture is always and unconditionally to be understood in the *plural*, as the various modes of being and doing of human existence. In this framework the idea of "advanced" or "retarded" cultures or histories is completely out of place. This is precisely because such a judgment necessarily and always surreptitiously privileges the cultural and historical context of Europe out of which it is being made.

Thus, Cabral's basic starting point necessarily presupposes the critique of any metaphysics of history (Kant, Hegel, Marx, etc.) which views human historicity as a singular and totalizing world-historical process. Cabral, for example, would be in categorical agreement with Castoriadis when the latter affirms that the European self-centered conception that "in truth, there is but one history and for all that matters, this one history coincides with our own," this view which sees European history as the truth of human history *as such* and as the " 'transcendentally obligatory' meeting point of all particular histories,"[54] this narrowly confined Eurocentric universe in which the West is still immersed, has to be concretely overcome.

Thus, for Cabral, given this theoretic framework, colonialism or any form of external subjugation is understood as the interruption of the historicity of the colonized.

> If we do not forget the historical perspective of the major events in the life of humanity, if, while maintaining due respect for all philosophies, we do not forget that the world is the creation of man himself, then colonialism can be considered as the paralysis or deviation or even the halting of the history of one people in favour of the acceleration of the historical development of other peoples.[55]

To the extent then that national liberation is the overcoming of the colonialist interruption of the historicity of the colonized, it is a process of returning "to the source" out of which the colonized spun their history prior to being colonized—i.e., thingified. In other words, the struggle against colonialism is a reaction to a presently frozen reality in terms of the suppressed possibilities of this reality itself. But what does this mean? Is it a going back to an archaic past? What is the "source" toward which the "return" is directed?

"Paralysis," "deviation," "halting" these are the terms used by Cabral to describe the actuality of colonialism. These terms suggest the interruption or blockage of a process whose patterns of unfolding do

not precede the actual process of unfolding itself. For what has been
halted is the lived life, the histories/cultures of the various African
communities which in their totality constitute the peoples of Africa.
In other words, this interruption itself has already been incorporated
as a specific historic event—the memory of a defeat, among other
things—in the lived actuality of those it subjugated.

What the colonized "might have been" had colonialism not occurred
is not a historically pertinent question, precisely because it posits and
presupposes, on the ontological level, a false dichotomy between history and the historicity of existence. Rather the central concern of the
"return to the source" is the drastic effect of this interruption and
the possibility of overcoming this negative inheritance of the African
present.

For Fanon as for Cabral the abstract affirmations and declarations
regarding the existence of a pre-colonial culture/history is not to the
point. What matters is to disclose a future out of what has endured
against colonialism and out of what European domination itself has
established in its historic African odyssey. Cabral fully recognizes the
impact of colonialism on African societies—the introduction of money,
the building of cities, the creation of new urban classes—but insists
that this is nothing more than the aberration of a people's history. To
be sure, the negative effects of this aberration can and do become part
of the positive historical reality of the colonized once decolonization
is actualized.

When the colonial situation as a whole is put in question, the negative
and negating experience of colonialism is then positively reappropriated and reclaimed. As Cabral puts it:

> In the colonized countries where colonization on the whole blocked
> the historical process of the development of the subjected peoples
> or else eliminated them radically or progressively, imperialist capital
> imposed new types of relationships on indigenous society, the struc-
> ture of which became more complex and it stirred up, fomented,
> poisoned or resolved contradictions and social conflicts; it intro-
> duced together with money and the development of internal and
> external markets, new elements in the economy, it brought about
> the birth of new nations from human groups or from peoples who
> were at different stages of historical development.[56]

In "blocking the historical process," which constitutes the historicity
of the indigenous populace, colonialism superimposes a different order

of historicity on the occupied territory. It thus brings about new historical circumstances "in favour of the acceleration of the historical development" of the colonizing society. The residue of these colonialist eventuations, which among other things have brought about the "birth of new nations," has resulted in a paradoxical reality divided unto itself as the actuality of contemporary Africa.

Instead of being organic wholes, these "new nations" are Euro-African hybrid constructions which do not arise out of the internal constancy of an indigenous historical formation. They are, furthermore, and in addition to the above, the amalgams of differing ethnic "human groups" without any internal or organic cohesion, either with each other or with the vertically superimposed hybrid construction. This then is the historical and political actuality created by colonialism and perpetuated by neocolonialism.

Within the confines of this situation the African past, "untouched" or minimally affected by colonialism, exists as a subordinated historical-cultural totality.

> Repressed, persecuted, humiliated, betrayed by certain social groups who have compromised with the foreign power, culture [history] took refuge in the villages, in the forests, and in the spirit of the victims of domination.[57]

In other words, colonialism brings about a double society in subordination: on the one hand, the rural mass who experience colonialism as an external limit and imposition, and on the other, those whose existence is directly tied to the new developments brought about by colonial conquest—i.e., the Westernized urban populace.

Such societies divided within themselves are impaired actualities for they do not have internal to themselves a common *ethos* that constitutes them as organic historic wholes. It is toward overcoming this truncation that the "return to the source" directs itself. This process of "return" is a cultural and political recovery of the suppressed historic possibilities in the existence of the colonized. Thus, the confrontation with colonialism assumes, as we have already seen with Fanon, the character and disposition of two distinct groups: the urban and rural native.

> A distinction must be made between the situation of the masses, who preserve their culture, and that of the social groups who are

assimilated or partially so, who are cut off [from the indigenous history] and culturally alienated.[58]

For Cabral, as for Fanon, this distinction is fundamental precisely because it dictates the specific direction, in terms of the anti-colonial struggle, that orients those assimilated and those negatively affected by the culture of the colonizing power.

The Westernized native turns toward the struggle for liberation only when confronted by the futility of his attempts at integration. In the compartmentalized actuality of the colonial setup this failure translates either into existence in a cultural limbo, or into a direct identification (engaged or abstract) with the subordinate rural mass.[59] For the rural mass, on the other hand, the conflict with colonialism is a lived actuality felt as an external confinement and imposition. In fact the beginning of the organized armed struggle is nothing more than the resumption of the conflict with the original intruders.

It is necessary to emphasize, at this point, that the conflict with colonialism does not initially arise as an effort to "return to the source." As we saw with Fanon, in like manner for Cabral, the "return to the source" arises out of the failure of the politics of the urban parties and is grounded on lived historical experience. In 1958–1959 in the cities and urban centers of Guinea-Bissau, Cabral and the PAIGC experienced this failure and it was by way of reorienting the struggle that the "return to the source" was established as the basic direction of the movement.[60]

This changing of direction was thus not a quest for an uncontaminated romantic past but a concrete practical effort grounded on the lived historic actualities of the struggle. This is how Cabral describes the sociological dynamic out of which it develops:

> It is within the framework of this daily drama [of marginal existence], against the backcloth of the usually violent confrontation between the mass of the people and the ruling colonial class that a feeling of bitterness or a *frustration complex* is bred and develops among the indigenous petite bourgeoisie [the urban native]. At the same time, they are becoming more and more conscious of a compelling need to question their marginal status, and to re-discover an identity. Thus they turn to the people around them, the people at the other extreme of the socio-cultural conflict—the native mass.[61]

This turning toward "the native mass," which is a *decision of conscience* is the first moment in the fusion of the urban and rural native.

The Westernized urban natives who join the anti-colonial eruption do so by rejecting their assimilation, their cultural indigence, and successfully indigenize themselves into the historicity of their people. In fact, as we have already seen, the reclaiming of one's indigenousness is, for the Westernized native, the originative moment of his anti-colonial commitment. It is the moment of a historical and existential decision, at which point the *assimilado* begins the cultural and historical metamorphosis that will positively reimmerse him into the historicity of the indigenous folk.[62]

This whole dynamic is thus a response to an existence of estranged marginality. It is a dialectic stimulated and provoked by colonialism which boomerangs by internally undermining the coherence of colonialist subjugation. It is not a futile attempt to dig out a purely African past and return to a dead tradition. Rather, it is the "denial" by the urban native of the cultural/historical supremacy of the "dominant power over that of the dominated people with which it must identify."[63]

In turning toward the rural native the Westernized urban native critically recognizes his own self-negated historical and cultural identity. Now, this self recognition—and the ambience of cultural anxiety in which it is generated—becomes a political and historical force only when it concretely annihilates itself as its own lived self-negation. When this happens (i.e., the "negation of the negation," in Marxist-Hegelian language) the "return to the source," beyond abstract cultural/political affirmations (*Africanité*, Pan-Africanism, etc.), becomes a lived historical and political actuality manifested in the national liberation struggle of a specific history and people.

> When the "return to the source" goes beyond the individual and is expressed through "groups" or "movements," the contradiction is transformed into struggle (secret or overt), and is a prelude to the pre-independence movement or of the struggle for liberation from the foreign yoke. So, the "return to the source" is of no historical importance unless it brings not only real involvement in the struggle for independence, but also complete and absolute identification with the hopes of the mass of the people, who contest not only the foreign culture but also the foreign domination as a whole.[64]

In order to truly grasp what Cabral means by the "return to the source," it is necessary at this point to examine the above formulations in some detail.

This "return" is not a return to tradition in its stasis. We are not, therefore, engaged in an antiquarian quest for an already existing authentic past. Rather, we are engaged in the affirmation by the Westernized native of the historicity of the rural indigenous mass. Simultaneously, this is the self-negation by the Westernized native of his own cultural legitimacy. The obverse of this denial is the positive affirmation of the stunted indigenous culture. This affirmation, furthermore, is not a theoretical/abstract assertion in need of proof. It is the "complete and absolute identification with the hopes" and aspirations of the dominated rural mass which is aimed at a joint process of struggle. It is, in other words, a practical and engaged affirmation which asserts what it struggles to institute: the historicity of the colonized. It is in this context that the reintegration of the Westernized native into the indigenous heritage comes about.

In "returning," the urban native brings with him the European cultural baggage that constitutes his person. He is a doctor, a student, an agronomist, a taxi driver, a skilled worker, etc., and thus brings, in the facticity of his Being, European values, skills, mannerisms, attitudes—lived aspects of European culture. The "complete and absolute identification" of the urban native is reciprocated by his acceptance and reintegration into the indigenous milieu. The Westernized native is appreciated for the skills and wider horizons that are incarnated in him. Simultaneously, in daily interaction in the midst of dire hardships and struggle, he comes to fully appreciate and value the resilience and elasticity (Nietzsche's "plastic power") of the indigenous history and culture—which, until recently, he saw as petrified and inert. As Cabral puts it:

> "petite bourgeoisie" (intellectuals, clerks) or the urban working class (workers, chauffeurs, salary-earners in general), having to live day by day with the various peasant groups in the heart of the rural population . . . discover at the grass roots the richness of their cultural values (philosophic, political, artistic, social and moral) . . . [and] realize, not without a certain astonishment, the richness of spirit, the capacity for reasoned discussion and clear exposition of ideas, the facility for understanding and assimilating concepts on the part of population groups who yesterday were forgotten, if not despised . . . by the colonizer and even by some nationals.[65]

European values and skills are thus absorbed into a new synthesis. This is possible because in embracing the indigenous historicity—in the very act of doing so—the Westernized native purges himself of the

Eurocentric frame that structures his consciousness. The "return" is thus a two-way process of cultural filtration and fertilization. In this dialectic European culture/history is recognized as a particular and *specific* disclosure of existence, aspects of which are retained or rejected in terms of the lived historicity and the practical requirements of the history that is being reclaimed.

Simultaneously, this process discards elements of the indigenous culture/history which are found to be antagonistic to the struggle.

> As we know, the armed liberation struggle requires the mobilization and organization of a significant majority of the population, the political and moral unity of the various social classes, the efficient use of modern arms and of other means of war, the progressive liquidation of the remnants of tribal mentality, and the rejection of social and religious rules and taboos which inhibit development of the struggle (gerontocracies, nepotism, social inferiority of women, rites and practices which are incompatible with the rational and national character of the struggle, etc.). The struggle brings about other profound modifications in the life of [the indigenous] populations. The armed liberation struggle implies, therefore, a veritable forced march along the road to cultural progress.[66]

The ossified African past—embodied in the rural native—is thus not preserved intact, but is cut and cast to fit the historic requirements of the struggle. Any aspect of tradition that hampers the concrete development of the movement is thus part of the *dead past* that must be sloughed off.

> Consider these features inherent in an armed liberation struggle: the practice of democracy, of criticism and self-criticism, the increasing responsibility of populations for the direction of their lives, literacy work, creation of schools and health services, training of cadres from peasant and worker backgrounds—and many other achievements.[67]

All of the above "achievements" which are indispensable for and constitute the success of the struggle as such require, as a prerequisite, a free and critical relation with the indigenous culture. A society in stasis cannot liberate itself. Liberation—"the practice of freedom"—requires a radical dialectic of mass participation and popular democracy.

From all that has just been said, it can be

concluded that in the framework of the conquest of national independence . . . the objectives must be at least the following: *development of a popular culture* and of all positive indigenous cultural values; *development of a national culture* based upon the history and the achievements of the struggle itself; constant promotion of the *political and moral awareness* of the people . . . to the cause of independence, of justice, and of progress; development of a technical, technological, and *scientific culture* . . . on the basis of a critical assimilation of man's achievements in the domains of art, science, literature. . . .[68]

In the process of undoing colonialism the colonized culture as colonized also undoes itself. It destroys the frozen and mummified forms of existence imposed on it. Thus, it should be clear by now that "the practice of freedom" is possible only within the context of "the return to the source" which is the internal structure of African self-emancipation.

Properly speaking, the "return" is the dialectic, internal to the African liberation struggle, which allows for the possibility of African freedom. As Cabral tells us—in keeping with Fanon—if in some form or other the "return" is not instituted as the actuality of the movement then the "struggle will have failed to achieve its objective."[69] This is so because the "return" is the liberation of the stunted possibilities of the colonized. It is within this context that, in a polemical encounter with dogmatic Marxism-Leninism, Cabral pointedly asserts that beyond historical "stages" and other such fashionable formulations what is at stake is the freeing of the "productive forces" of the colonized.

The struggle is not aimed at a certain "stage" nor is it directed by or toward a given pre-established "ideology." Its only theoretic concerns are the possibilities opened up by the struggle itself which are properly explored and articulated as its own grounded self-awareness.[70] Thus, national liberation, affirms Cabral, "exists only when the national productive forces have been completely freed from every kind of foreign domination."[71] We need now to examine what the term "productive forces" means in Cabral's usage.

The "productive forces," a technical term borrowed from orthodox Marxism, does not refer to the relations and forces of production in the strict economic sense. Rather, it refers to the sum total of cultural resources that constitutes a people in the open-ended process of its historical becoming. The term "productive forces" is thus a formulation which is inclusive of, but not exclusive to, the economic realities of the colonized.[72]

It is in this context that Cabral confronts the Eurocentrism of Marxist conceptions of history, class, and class struggle. In other words, "this leads us to pose the question: does history begin only with the development of the phenomenon of 'class,' and consequently of class struggle?" To give an affirmative reply to this foundational question is to place "various human groups in Africa, Asia and Latin America . . . outside of history, at the time when they were subjected to the yoke of imperialism."[73] It is, in other words, to justify European conquest.

Anterior to the history of class and class struggles and serving as its ontological underpinning we have, for Cabral, the "productive forces" of a human group—the material/historical disclosive and creative situation of human existence. It is this reality that manifests itself in the formation of classes and the dynamics of the class struggle in the history of specific peoples. The "history of class struggles" conceived as a world-historical totalizing process, as Marx understands it in the *Communist Manifesto*, is a specific ontic manifestation—peculiar to the historicity of European modernity—of this ontological fact, which Marx universalizes and ontologizes as the historicity of human existence *in toto*. Addressing himself specifically to this point Cabral states:

> There is a preconception . . . that imperialism made us enter history at the moment when it began its *adventures* in our countries. This preconception must be denounced: for somebody on the left, and for Marxists in particular, history is the history of the class struggle. Our opinion is exactly the contrary. We consider that when imperialism arrived in Guinea it made us leave history—*our* history. We agree that history in our country is the result of class struggle, but we have *our own* class struggle in our country; the moment . . . colonialism arrived it made us leave *our* history and enter *another* history.[74]

The reality of colonialism is thus the violent superimposition of European historicity on African historicity. It is, in other words, the truncation or paralysis of the dominated "productive forces." In this context national liberation is the freeing of these "productive forces"—the reintroduction of the colonized into history.[75]

Against the history of an "adventure" Cabral counterposes "our" history and "our own" struggles, which are interior to the specific historicity of the indigenous folk. Once this fundamental and axiomatic premise is accepted, then the struggle can properly be understood as a concrete attempt to solve problems peculiar to specific histories. In a "Brief Analysis of the Social Structure of Guinea," Cabral gives us a concrete example of what this means.[76]

In this text we are presented with a systematic analysis of the various cultures and ethnic groups that collectively constitute Guinea-Bissau. The aim of the text is not to force Marxist (or any other) categories or justify an *a priori* schema of how a liberation struggle should unfold. Rather, the text is descriptive and concerned with the various egalitarian-horizontal and hierarchical ethnic communities, their internal social-economic-political structures, the position of women, their relation to the land, the history of relations (hostile or friendly) that each particular ethnic group has with other ethnic groups and with the Portuguese, and how this relates (if it does) to the group's particular mode of life and political organization.

Regarding the urban centers, the analysis is concerned with locating those groups that are susceptible to the call of the movement and those who give it a deaf ear, and in each case locating the reasons (historical or sociological) why this is the case. In both the rural and urban contexts, Cabral's analysis is descriptive and explorative of the concrete possibilities imbedded in this context. It takes its theoretic cues and suggestions from the lived situation with which and in which it is engaged.

Thus, against fashionable dogmas and "theories of revolution," the "return to the source" is a concrete assessment of one's *own* lived historicity. To "have ideology [theory]," says Cabral, "doesn't necessarily mean that you have to define whether you are a communist, socialist, or something like that. To have ideology is to know what you want in your own condition."[77] It should be noted that Cabral's descriptive presentation in "Brief Analysis of the Social Structure of Guinea" parallels, in its basic direction, Fanon's discussion of the Algerian situation in *L'An Cinq de la Révolutione Algérienne.* Instead of mimicking Fanon's analysis, Cabral does for Guinea what Fanon did for Algeria: he engages in a distinct and hence novel theoretic assessment of a specific historical situation. Thus "to know what you want in your condition" is to have a concrete theoretic understanding of one's lived historical situation. For both Fanon and Cabral, then, theory, properly speaking, is always the concrete hermeneutics or interpretation of the needs and requirements of a specific historicity.[78] Their theoretic labors are focused on an engaged hermeneutics of their lived situation.

This knowledge, furthermore, arises from and is grounded in the exigencies specific to a particular history at a particular moment of its self-unfolding. As already noted, the "return" is directed toward creating the socio-historical context in which "the practice of freedom" becomes the lived actuality of a formerly colonized people. Indeed, this is what it means to triumph over colonialism or neocolonialism: to reinstitute the world of the colonized beyond the residues of conquest.[79]

As Cabral categorically affirms:

> Ten years ago [before the struggle], we were Fula, Mandjak, Mandinka, Balante, Pepel, and others. Now we are a nation of Guineans.[80]

To the extent that it is successful, the struggle effectively transforms those who through it secure their freedom. As Fanon tells us, the struggle sublates "old beliefs and friendships from the time *before life began.*"[81] This is so precisely because it inaugurates a new life. "Ten years ago," "before life began," the people of Guinea-Bissau were differing ethnic groups forcefully imprisoned within the confines of Portuguese colonial subjugation. "Now we are a nation of Guineans," a nation created in the active pursuit of autonomy and freedom.

III

In both Fanon and Cabral we see the thinking of a synthesis of traditional and modern aspects of African society in the context of actualizing the possibilities of the African liberation struggle. This thinking, furthermore, is inscribed at a fundamental level with democratic values and aspirations. Indeed, for both of these thinkers the effort of thought is directed at articulating the process of liberation as the self-formation of African nation states from out of the confines of the former colonial territories.

The patriotism or nationalism on which such a metamorphosis is grounded is, furthermore, a multiethnic national awareness arising from the recognition of difference and the establishment of a common history of emancipatory struggle. In fact each former colony as an independent state is an aggregate of ethnic groups. Thus, we have an *inclusive* and emancipatory nationalism in contradistinction to an *exclusive* and retrograde nationalism.[82]

Indeed, as Césaire put it, "our liberation placed us on the left."[83] Or, as Sartre reminds us, "colonialism creates the patriotism of the colonized."[84] This is a patriotism that derives from the "hermeneutical situation . . . of the formerly colonized, the oppressed . . . struggling for more justice and equality."[85] It is the patriotism of those who reclaim their historical existence in terms of and by reference to the historicity of the values inscribed in the charter of the United Nations,[86] a nationalism grounded in the recognition that *difference* is what constitutes the concrete existence of each nation state and people in their particular and specific historicity. This is what I referred to, in the first chapter of this study, as the basis for global earthly solidarity.[87]

To think through the historicity of lived existence, this is what Fanon and Cabral do from within their lived situatedness in the African liberation struggle. In their work, African philosophical hermeneutics finds a living example of its vocation. Thus, in terms of contemporary concerns—political, economic, scientific, cultural, etc.—the hermeneutics of African philosophy must engage in situated reflections aimed at the pragmatic and practical aim of enhancing the lived actuality of post-colonial Africa. It is only in this way that African philosophy, as the reflexive hermeneutics of its own historicalness, can grow and cultivate itself as a concrete contemporary philosophic discourse.[88]

As Marcien Towa puts it, African philosophic thought is deeply committed to an

> auto-centric Africa which is the center of its own conceptions, of its decisions and the actualization of the totality of its spheres of essential activity: political, economic and spiritual; a fraternal Africa, which will respect this same auto-centric principle as it applies to itself and as it applies to other peoples.[89]

Indeed, an "auto-centric Africa"! The effort to theoretically assist in the actualizing of such a possibility is, for African philosophy, a noble and worthwhile cause. Furthermore, as we have seen in our explorations of Fanon and Cabral, this is the continuation of the age-old African struggle to reclaim, beyond colonialism and neocolonialism, the existence and historicity of contemporary Africa.

> To enslave [i.e., colonize] a people means to contain [or restrict] them to activities which do not serve their needs, but someone else's, for an end [or purpose] which is not theirs, but someone else's. The enslaved people is thus inserted, as a mere instrument, into a practical process whose movements and goals remain alien and unknown to it. Hence, the culture produced is not their own, but someone else's. The enslavement of a people dries up its culture at its source.[90]

Taking the negativity of this situation as its immediate background and source or point of departure, African philosophy aims at reviving the cultural and historical actuality of the formerly colonized/enslaved peoples of Africa.

As we have seen in this chapter, Fanon and Cabral, in their theoretic articulations cultivate a radical hermeneutics of the colonized in the process of self-emancipation. This then is the concrete and practical example that African philosophy must follow in its own engaged musings and reflexive reflections. In so doing it will explicitly constitute itself as a radical and emancipatory African philosophical hermeneutics.

Consciously and in a critical and rigorous manner, it will appropriate and add to the practical and engaged theoretic heritage of the African liberation struggle. In so doing it will become a radical and emancipatory hermeneutic inventory of our post-colonial African inheritance.[91] For as Foucault tells us: "philosophy is precisely the challenging of all phenomena of domination at whatever level or under whatever form they present themselves—political, economic, sexual, institutional, and so on."[92]

Conclusion
Africa in the Present Context
of Philosophy

Man aspires to know truth and the hidden things of nature, but this endeavour is difficult and can only be attained with great labour and patience. . . . Hence people hastily accept what they have heard from their fathers and shy from any [critical] examination.

—Zar'a Ya'aqob
Sixteenth-century Abyssinian philosopher

In philosophy, the end is the synoptic recapitulation of the whole.[1] Thus, by way of a conclusion, I will present a brief overview of what this study has hoped to achieve. In so doing I will locate and stake out, within the framework of contemporary thought, a critical position in terms of the question of what African philosophy—in the last decade of the twentieth century—can and should be. This will reflexively specify my own position in the ongoing discourse of contemporary African philosophy.

That such a thing exists is beyond dispute. What needs to be done is to preliminarily trace out its theoretic role in the present situation of the continent. For the effort to appropriate the historic and emancipatory possibilities of our post-colonial present is—as argued in this study—the compelling theoretic and moral responsibility of African philosophic work.

I

The introduction abstractly articulated the basic premise and grounding thesis of the study as a whole: that philosophy is inherently

117

and in its very nature a hermeneutics of the existentiality of human existence. This was done by exploring, in a preliminary manner, the contemporary actuality of the debate in African philosophy.

By way of substantiating the above, chapter 1 queried the relation of philosophic reflection to the actuality out of which it constitutes itself. In like manner, chapter 2 explicated this historicity further by critically engaging the failings of contemporary African philosophic thought in terms of its thematic relations to the discourse of the African liberation struggle.

Thus, the first half of the study provided a metaphilosophic attestation to the hermeneuticity of contemporary African philosophic thought. The second half of the study, on the other hand, presented a hermeneutics of the possibility of African freedom focused on the violence and the emancipatory hopes and possibilities of the African liberation struggle.

Beyond the disputes and squabbles of Ethnophilosophy and its "Professional" critics, chapters 3 and 4 presented substantial philosophic explorations of questions that pertain to the actualities and possibilities of the present. Through all of the above, this study has presented African philosophy as a critical hermeneutics of the African situation. In its specific arguments and formulations this study has been grounded in the concrete awareness that philosophy in general and African philosophy in particular is, above all else and necessarily, a hermeneutical thinking through of its own lived historicalness.

By taking Fanon's and Cabral's work as paradigmatic for African philosophy, I have argued that the hermeneutics of African philosophy is, in effect, a situated emancipatory thinking akin to the theoretic labors of these two leaders of and participants in the African liberation struggle. In their work African philosophical hermeneutics finds its paradigmatic forerunners. Where then is this situated thinking located within the larger framework of contemporary thought?

II

As Theophilus Okere has convincingly argued, the "historicity and relativity of truth—and this always means truth as we can and do attain it—is one of the main insights of the hermeneutical revolution"[2] in contemporary thought, which substantiates and in turn is substantiated by the efforts embodied in African philosophic discourse. Indeed, contemporary African philosophy is an articulation from within, and in terms of the exigencies of the African world, of the prevalent ascendance of context-oriented modes of philosophizing in the discipline as a whole. In this context, as Fanon puts it:

> Universality resides in this decision to recognize and accept the reciprocal relativism of different cultures [and histories], once the colonial status is irreversibly excluded.[3]

Contemporary African philosophy, in this regard, originating as it does out of the "heart of darkness," is an added critical questioning voice in the varied current discourses of philosophy. It is the questioning voice of those whom the modern European world compelled into voicelessness in the process of its own violent and self-righteous establishment. As Outlaw puts it:

> In light of the European incursion into Africa, the emergence of "African philosophy" poses deconstructive (and reconstructive) challenges.[4]

The "deconstructive challenge" of African philosophy is directed at the Eurocentric residue inherited from colonialism. The institutional structures that the "independent" states of Africa have taken over from their former colonizers—the grounding parameters and cultural codes inscribed in these political, economic, educational, and social organizations—remain, in their essential constitution, oriented by colonial and European condescending attitudes. In every respect these vital societal structures remain unthought and unchanged. Thus, the unmasking and undoing of this Eurocentric residue on the level of theory is a basic task and challenge for African philosophic thought.

Conversely, and in conjunction with the above, the "reconstructive challenge" of African philosophy is aimed at supplying a positive hermeneutic supplement to the concrete efforts under way on the continent. It is an indigenizing theoretic effort in the service of revitalizing the historicity of African existence within the context and the bounds of our contemporary world. Paraphrasing Ngugi wa Thiong'o, one can say that this is the process of "decolonizing the mind"[5] or, with Cabral, as we saw in chapter 4, one can describe it as the struggle to "return to the source."

In this theoretic double venture, the hermeneutics of African philosophy finds itself allied with the various and varied critical voices that constitute the contemporary intellectual panorama. As Edward Said has observed, in this panorama,

> the real issue is whether indeed there can be a true representation of anything, or whether any and all representations, because they are representations, are embedded first in the language and then in the culture, institutions, and political ambience of the representer. If the latter alternative is the correct one (as I believe it is), then we must be prepared to accept the fact that a representation is *eo ipso* implicated, intertwined, embedded, interwoven with a great many other things besides the "truth," which is itself a representation. What this must lead us to methodologically is to view representations (or misrepresentations—the distinction is at best a matter of degree) as inhabiting a common field of play defined for them, not by some inherent common subject matter alone, but by some common history, tradition, [and] universe of discourse.[6]

This then is what I have argued, in this study as a whole, from within the problematic of philosophical hermeneutics and in terms of the basic character of African philosophy. Thus, in full awareness of its own lived situatedness and starting from it, African philosophical hermeneutics is engaged in articulating the *truth* of its lived present. This "truth" is, furthermore, nothing more than its own reflexive self-representation on the plane of philosophy, in the service of fulfilling the emancipatory hopes and aspirations inscribed in our "common history, tradition, [and] universe of discourse" as post-colonial Africans. This then is, in my view, the sense and meaning of the "post-" in "postcolonial"[7] as it relates to contemporary African philosophic thought and practice.

Now more than ever, at the end of the twentieth century, we contemporary Africans engaged in philosophy have to undertake the practice of our discipline in full awareness of its limits, implications, and possibilities. Hermes rendered the messages of the gods; in our context, this is the service of deciphering and interpreting the sense of our mortal existence within the bounds of the present post-colonial situation. The hope of this study has thus been to contribute its efforts toward the augmentation of this cumulative and worthwhile project. For this is the calling and duty of African philosophical hermeneutics.

In this interpretative service *we* will contribute our share in consummating the self-emancipation of Africa. In so doing we will acknowledge and partake of the process of repaying our collective debt to those whose sacrifice and hard struggle actualized our freedom. For ultimately—when all is said and done—this is the ethical, political, and existential impulse of African philosophic thought.

> For a long time, in the night, his voice was that of the voiceless phantoms of his ancestors, whom he had raised up. With them, he wept their death; but also, in long cadence, they sang his birth.[8]

Notes

Introduction

All emphasis in the original unless otherwise indicated.

1 *The Epic of Gilgamesh*, ed., int. by N. K. Sanders (New York: Penguin Books, 1980).

2 If one looks at Homer, Hesiod, the Sumerian epic of Gilgamesh, and the West African epic of Sundiata—and I am sure this observation can be verified in terms of additional myths from other parts and peoples of the world—it is clear that, despite their many differences, all these texts articulate their discourse from within the limits of human finitude. In all four, the mythological narrative never threatens the compass of human mortality within which it unfolds, and all the fantastic deeds that involve and even implicated the gods occur. As is well known, starting from Plato, in the tradition of Greek and later European metaphysics, the effort of philosophy—except for the "dark horses" of the tradition—is directly aimed at doing precisely this: overcoming the limits of human finitude. Among the Platonic dialogues the *Phaedo* is the best illustration of this basic and grounding orientation in European metaphysics. In this regard—commenting on Edmund Husserl, an influential exponent of this orientation toward human finitude—Jacques Derrida writes that, for Husserl "death is recognized as but an empirical and extrinsic signification, a worldly accident." *Speech and Phenomena* (Evanston: Northwestern University Press, 1973), p. 10. To my knowledge, however, the strongest statement of this perspective is Hegel's assertion that "logic [i.e., his *Logic*] is to be understood as the system of pure reason, as the realm of pure thought. . . . It can therefore be said that this content is the exposition of God as he is in his eternal essence before the creation of nature and of finite mind." *Hegel's Science of Logic*, trans. A. V. Miller (New York: Humanities Press, 1976), p. 50. In contrast to this kind of "infinite thinking" hermeneutics enunciates a "finite" descriptive kind of thinking, which is grounded in the inherently interpretative and mortal character of human existence as such. This is the kind of thinking or human wisdom—the knowledge of our own limitedness—that the Socrates of the *Apology* claimed for himself in contradistinction to the Sophists.

3 Drew A. Hyland, *The Origins of Philosophy* (New York: Capricorn Books, 1973), p. 24.

4   Henry Odera Oruka, "African Philosophy: A Brief Personal History and Current Debate," in *Contemporary Philosophy: A New Survey*, vol. 5, *African Philosophy*, ed. Guttorm Floistad (Dordrecht: Martinus Nijhoff, 1987), see especially pp. 46–55. For a recent discussion of the contemporary situation in African philosophy, see Fidelis U. Okafor, "Issues in African Philosophy Reexamined," *International Philosophical Quarterly*, vol. 33, no. 1, issue no. 129 (March 1993). See also Lucius Outlaw, "African, African American, Africana Philosophy," *The Philosophical Forum*, vol. 29, nos. 1–3 (Fall–Spring 1992–93).

5   Lucius Outlaw, "African 'Philosophy': Deconstructive and Reconstructive Challenges," *Contemporary Philosophy: A New Survey*, vol. 5, *African Philosophy*, ed. Guttorm Floistad (Dordrecht: Martinus Nijhoff, 1987). In this same anthology, see also Henry Odera Oruka, "African Philosophy: A Brief Personal History and Current Debate."

6   Martin Heidegger, "The Age of the World View," in *The Question concerning Technology* (New York: Harper & Row, 1977), p. 116.

7   Kwasi Wiredu, "On Defining African Philosophy," *African Philosophy: The Essential Readings*, ed., int. by Tsenay Serequeberhan (New York: Paragon House, 1991), p. 88.

8   The label "Professional Philosophy" is the self-designation of the above-named four African philosophers and refers to the fact that, at some level, they all share a modernist bias in terms of which their respective views in and on African philosophy are articulated. In this regard, see Henry Odera Oruka, "Four Trends in Current African Philosophy," *Philosophy in the Present Situation of Africa*, ed. Alwin Diemer (Wiesbaden: Franz Steiner Verlag Gmbh, 1981), specifically note 15, p. 7. The following are the main texts of Professional Philosophy: Wiredu, *Philosophy and An African Culture* (Cambridge: Cambridge University Press, 1980); Hountondji, *African Philosophy, Myth and Reality* (Bloomington: Indiana University Press, 1983); Bodunrin, "Which Kind of Philosophy for Africa," *Philosophy in the Present Situation of Africa*, ed. Alwin Diemer (Wiesbaden: Franz Steiner Verlag Gmbh, 1981); and Oruka, *Sage Philosophy* (New York: E. J. Brill, 1990). The above texts are mostly compilations and collections of papers published by their respective authors in the 1960s, 1970s and 1980s. As indicated above, "Ethnophilosophy" is a derogatory term coined by Hountondji in 1969 (ibid., p. 34). It has also been used in the contemporary debate to refer without disparagement to ethnographic work in African philosophy. One last point: In my last very pleasant and fruitful meeting with Kwasi Wiredu, at the Central Division APA meeting in Louisville, Kentucky (April 24–26, 1992), he very strenuously, but cordially, objected to my portrayal and characterization of his position in African philosophy. For the record I repeat now what I then expressed to him verbally, that my representation of his views is based on his published work and specifically on his book, *Philosophy and an African Culture*. In all fairness to Wiredu, I would also like to note that his most recent views, both oral and written, are not, properly speaking, in keeping with the historically originative position of Professional Philosophy as portrayed above. In this regard my remarks apply only to his book, *Philosophy and an African Culture*, and to his articles on this subject that precede the publication of the above-indicated book.

9   In this regard see the "classic" statement of this Eurocentric/modernist view in Hountondji, *African Philosophy, Myth and Reality*, p. 66. On this point Lucius Outlaw correctly points out that:

As Hountondji plays out his argument it quickly unravels. It takes only a few probing questions to uncover the fact that Hountondji uses "African" as a signifier not just for *geographical* origins, but also for race/ethnicity. This attempt to circumscribe "African" is frustrated by the play of forces that brings on a deconstructive encounter with the "white mythology" infecting Philosophy. At the core of this mythology is a substance-accident metaphysics grounding a supplemental philosophical anthropology: the soul, consciousness, or the person is regarded as the *essence* of the human being; their race, ethnicity, or gender is secondary or accidental. This is at best naive. No living [or dead] person is accidentally or secondarily African or European, that is to say, is of a particular race or ethnicity "accidentally" while being a "person" or "human" *substantially*. ("African 'Philosophy': Deconstructive and Reconstructive Challenges," p. 34)

At this point it should be noted that Hountondji has—since his original formulation in 1973—presented a defense of his original position which begrudgingly and very slightly qualifies its style if not its content. In fact his defense is a forceful and more vigorous restatement of his original position. My view of Hountondji's qualified position rests on a reading of his paper "Occidentalism, Elitism: Answer to Two Critiques," which appeared in *Quest*, an international African journal of philosophy, vol. 3, no. 2 (December 1989); for the original French version, see *Recherche, Pedagogie et Culture*, Paris, no. 56 (January–March 1982). Since an author is usually consulted, by way of requesting permission when his work is presented in translation, I must assume that this piece represents his latest view, which is not substantially different from his original position. In any case, I am restating Hountondji's original position precisely because I am interested in laying out the overall original situation, in contradistinction to which the hermeneutical orientation in contemporary African philosophy was initially constituted. On this last point please see the remarks to note 10. For a different and more sympathetic reading of Hountondji's qualified position, please see Kwame Anthony Appiah, *In My Father's House* (New York: Oxford University Press, 1992). As Appiah puts it: "Hountondji has—for example, in a talk at the African Literature Association meeting in Dakar, Senegal, in April 1989—accepted this point, insisting now that his original *prise de position* was *polemical*. In a situation where African philosophy was supposed to be exhausted by a descriptive ethnophilosophy, it is understandable that his point—that this was by no means all there was to philosophy—was overstated, as the claim that ethnophilosophy had nothing to do with philosophy" (p. 203, note 47).

10 On this point, see Hountondji, *African Philosophy, Myth and Reality*, part one, section one, "An Alienated Literature."

11 Theophilus Okere, *African Philosophy: A Historico-Hermeneutical Investigation of the Conditions of Its Possibility* (Lanham, Md.: University Press of America, 1983), p. viii. Regarding this reference I would like to point out that, while being in complete agreement with Okere on most everything, I find this reference partially problematic. The reference in question reads: "Somewhere in between, on the one hand, the chauvinism of those who claim that philosophy is of its nature a treasure hidden in the secret recesses of highest Olympus inaccessible to non-westerners [i.e., Professional Philosophy], and on the other the *a priori* claims of those who think that philosophy is so natural a thing that if the Greeks had it at all, all people

and, therefore, Africans must already have it [i.e., Ethnophilosophy], this essay finds its place." What I find problematic in this statement is that it uncritically accepts the view advocated by Professional Philosophy that, prior to the modern age Africa was innocent of philosophy as such. Okere fails to note that, on good hermeneutic grounds (and leaving the methodological naiveté of Ethnophilosophy and of Oruka's *Sage Philosophy* aside) the foundational wondering and musing of traditional African sages have—in their continuous critical and safeguarding relation to the traditions (i.e., the ethnic world-views) they inhabit—a hermeneutic and philosophic function. To this extent, it has to be conceded in principle that their reflections and intellectual productions are products of philosophic effort. The alternative would be to say that the countless and intricate African world-views that we have inherited beyond the castrating experience of colonialism, have been preserved and perpetuated without the mediative and critical effort of human thought. But can tradition be transmitted without the critical mediating effort of thought? And isn't this kind of thought inherently philosophic, inasmuch as it is concerned with the perpetuation and the transmission of the existential actuality of a lived and living heritage? To be sure, along with philosophy, one will also find other kinds of intellectual products: myth, art, music—these, however, do not in any way nullify, by their presence, the actuality of philosophic thought in their midst as the *grounding vision* of their distinct specificity. How these differing intellectual activities and products are differentiated is an issue we need not pursue at the present moment. One last point: Okere's book was first produced in 1971 as a doctoral dissertation at the *Institute Superior de Philosophie* of the Catholic University of Louvain and as V. Y. Mudimbe points out, its main and lofty merit is that of having inaugurated the hermeneutical orientation in the discourse of contemporary African philosophy ("African Gnosis: Philosophy and the Order of Knowledge," *African Studies Review*, vol. 28, nos. 2/3 [June/September 1985], pp. 210–11). As a pioneer Okere is thus, unbeknownst to himself, implicated, on this particular, in the views and positions he critically overcomes. Rarely does a pioneer escape such backlash!

12 Kwame Gyekye, *An Essay on African Philosophical Thought* (Cambridge: Cambridge University Press, 1987), p. 11.

13 Ibid., p. 43.

14 Okere, *African Philosophy, A Historico-Hermeneutical Investigation*, chapter five, "Philosophy and Non-Philosophy: Lessons from the History of Philosophy," pp. 81–113. For Okere's discussion of the historicity of African philosophy, see pp. 114–31 and specifically p. 121.

15 Frantz Fanon, *Towards the African Revolution* (New York: Grove Press, 1967), p. 23.

16 Amilcar Cabral, *Return to the Source: Selected Speeches* (New York: Monthly Review Press, 1973), *passim*, and specifically, p. 63. It is of the utmost importance to keep in mind that the phrase "return to the source" is *not* meant to suggest a "return" to a primordial "truth" or some uncontaminated "African *arche*"—as if this were possible or even desirable! As Cabral emphatically points out in the texts cited above, what is to be returned to and critically appropriated is the vigor, vitality (life), and ebullience of African existence which is reawakened by the anticolonial struggle. In other words, it is the reignited historicity of lived existence—

not the relics of a dead past—that is the "source" to which the "return" is directed by the lived exigencies of the present moment of history. In this regard Cabral's formulation is akin to Martin Heidegger's notion of *wieder-holen* (repetition), as it pertains to *Dasein*'s (i.e., the actuality of human existence) historicality. *Being and Time* (New York: Harper & Row, 1962), p. 437.

17   Marcien Towa, "Conditions for the Affirmation of a Modern African Philosophical Thought," *African Philosophy: The Essential Readings*, p. 192.

18   For Senghor's own defensive remarks regarding this rather controversial, if not obscene, statement, see "The Spirit of Civilization or the Laws of African Negro Culture," *Presence Africaine*, nos. 8–10 (June–November 1956), p. 52. For a more recent and very sympathetic reading of Senghor's perspective, see Olusegun Gbadegesin, "Negritude and Its Contribution to the Civilization of the Universal: Leopold Senghor and the Question of Ultimate Reality and Meaning," *Ultimate Reality and Meaning*, Interdisciplinary studies in the philosophy of understanding (Canadian journal), vol. 14, no. 1 (March 1991). On this point see also: Lucius Outlaw, "African 'Philosophy': Deconstructive and Reconstructive Challenges," pp. 26–32, and Abiola Irele, *The African Experience in Literature and Ideology* (Bloomington: Indiana University Press, 1990), pp. 67–124. For a systematic de-structuring of Senghor's notion of Négritude see chapter 2 of this study.

19   Towa, "Conditions for the Affirmation of a Modern African Philosophical Thought," p. 193.

20   Ibid., p. 191.

21   Ibid., p. 194.

22   Ibid., pp. 194–95.

23   Antonio Gramsci, *Prison Notebooks*, ed., trans. Q. Hoare and G. N. Smith (New York: International Publishers, 1975), p. 345.

24.   Aimé Césaire, *Return to My Native Land* (New York: Penguin Books, 1969), p. 88.

25   Kwame Anthony Appiah, "Is the Post- in Postmodernism the Post-in Postcolonial?" *Critical Inquiry*, vol. 17, no. 2 (Winter 1991), p. 353. This paper is now chapter seven of Appiah's important book, *In My Father's House*.

26   Amilcar Cabral, "The national movements of the Portuguese colonies," the opening address at the CONCP conference held in Dar-Es-Salaam 1965, collected in *Revolution in Guinea: Selected Texts* (New York: Monthly Review Press, 1969), p. 80.

27   Frantz Fanon, *The Wretched of the Earth* (New York: Grove Press, 1968), p. 316. Cabral expresses substantially the same view in "Connecting the Struggle: An Informal Talk with Black Americans," *Return to the Source: Selected Speeches* (New York: Monthly Review Press, 1973), pp. 75–92, *passim*.

28   Cornel West, *Prophesy Deliverance!* (Philadelphia: Westminster Press, 1982), p. 24. West makes this point in reference to African-American intellectuals and their work. The relevant sentence reads: "In fact, ironically, the attempt by black intellectuals to escape from their Americanness and even go beyond Western thought is itself very *American*." In the context of contemporary African philosophy, one needs only to substitute "European" for "American" and "African intellectuals"

for "black intellectuals" to see the relevance of this sentence for the discussion developed thus far in this introduction.

29 Frantz Fanon, *Black Skins, White Masks* (New York: Grove Press, 1967), p. 12. On this point for Cabral, see "Brief Analysis of the Social Structure in Guinea," *Revolution in Guinea: Selected Texts* (New York: Monthly Review Press, 1969).

30 For examples of what this means please see my papers, "Karl Marx and African Emancipatory Thought: A Critique of Marx's Euro-Centric Metaphysics," *Praxis International*, vol. 10, nos. 1/2 (April and July 1990), and "The Idea of Colonialism in Hegel's *Philosophy of Right*," *International Philosophical Quarterly*, vol. 29, no. 3, issue no. 115 (September 1989). See also, Emmanuel Eze, "On Modern and Mythic Worldviews: Thinking with and against Habermas," *Conference, A Journal of Philosophy*, vol. 1, no. 2 (Fall 1990). In my view this process of challenging the universalistic claims of Western philosophy is and should be an ongoing destructive concern of contemporary African philosophic thought which it will have to necessarily develop in the process of establishing and consolidating its own theoretic positions. It could not be otherwise, furthermore, precisely because European culture—philosophy included—historically and thematically establishes itself by radically differentiating itself from barbarism—the Otherness of the Other—the paradigmatic case of which is the Black African.

1. Philosophy and Post-colonial Africa

All emphasis in the original unless otherwise indicated.

1 Theophilus Okere, *African Philosophy: A Historico-Hermeneutical Investigation of the Conditions of Its Possibility* (Lanham, Md.: University Press of America, 1983), p. vii. See also, Elungu Pene Elungu, "La philosophie, condition du developpement en Afrique aujourd'hui," *Presence Africaine*, no. 103, 3d quarterly (1977), p. 3.

2 Marcien Towa, "Conditions for the Affirmation of a Modern African Philosophical Thought," in *African Philosophy: The Essential Readings*, ed. Tsenay Serequeberhan (New York: Paragon House, 1991), p. 187.

3 Frantz Fanon, *Towards the African Revolution* (New York: Grove Press, 1988), p. 120.

4 Unlike most others, as early as 1961 in his seminal work *The Wretched of the Earth* (New York: Grove Press, 1968), Fanon had pointed out the class and historico-political difficulties that lay ahead for the African anti-colonial struggle. In this regard see particularly the section titled, "The Pitfalls of National Consciousness." On this point Kofi Buenor Hadjor, a one time press aide in the publicity secretariat of the Nkrumah government, pays tribute to Fanon's keen insight at the time of his exile with Nkrumah in Guinea Conakry. "It was in Conakry that I first read Fanon, especially his *Wretched of the Earth* which my exile companion, John K. Tettegah, now Ghana's ambassador to the Soviet Union, gave me as a present. It did not take me long to realize that Fanon's analysis had much more to offer than Machiavelli and many of the other classics. Tettegah and I literally devoured the chapter on "The Pitfalls of National Consciousness" as we felt its analysis was too true to the Ghanaian situation." *On Transforming Africa Discourses with Africa's Leaders* (Trenton, N.J.: Africa World Press, 1987), p. 3.

5 Notice that this last sentence projects an African future that will "recognize" in our immediate post-colonial past the disappointments of the hopes and aspirations of the African liberation movement. In so doing it projects into the future the validity of its own assumptions given the situatedness of its own hermeneutical actuality. Now this "recognition" is not the "recognition" of some "objective state of affairs in the future," much less a prediction of what is to come. Rather it is a "recognition" that will be possible or will be possiblized only if the disappointed objectives of the African liberation struggle—yet to be explored in this text—are fulfilled (at least in part and in some way) in the future the sentence projects and on which it stakes its emancipatory hopes. In other words, if the neocolonial present endures into the immediate and remote future of Africa, all of the above will be no more than unfulfilled and lost possibilities of African historical existence.

6 Enrique Dussel, *Philosophy of Liberation* (New York: Orbis Books, 1985), p. 13.

7 This is the basic theme of George Bush's first presidency, the beginning of the "second American century" as he put it in his inaugural address. With the collapse of the Soviet Union (the other superpower) and its Eastern European allies, Bush, in keeping with the rhetoric of his predecessor, has claimed all of these developments as victories for what has come to be known as the Reagan-Bush conservative revolution in contemporary American politics. The August 2, 1990 Iraqi invasion of Kuwait, and the "100 hour" Gulf War unleashed by the United States of America on Iraq (in conjunction with and in the guise of the United Nations) starting January 16, 1991—all these developments are, by accident or design, framing the character of this "new world order" as extremely bellicose for the non-European world as a whole. American/Occidental military might, as in the days of old, seems to be, in a much more intense manner, the standard of "justice" in this "new world order." In this regard see, Noam Chomsky " 'What We Say Goes': The Middle East in the New World Order," *Z Magazine* (May 1991); Edward W. Said, "Ignorant Armies Clash by Night," *The Nation*, February 11, 1991; Anton Shammas, "A Lost Voice," *The New York Times Magazine*, April 28, 1991; and Eqbal Ahmad, "The Hundred-Hour War," *Dawn*, March 17, 1991.

8 Basil Davidson and Antonio Bronda, *Cross Roads in Africa* (Nottingham, Eng.: Spokesman Press, 1980), p. 36.

9 Ibid.

10 Hans-Georg Gadamer, *Truth and Method* (New York: Crossroad Publishers, 1982), pp. 158–59.

11 Ibid., second part, section I: "Schleiermacher's Project of a Universal Hermeneutics," *passim.*

12 *Hegel: The Difference between The Fichtean and Schellingian Systems of Philosophy*, trans. Dr. Jere Paul Surber (Atascadero, Calif.: Ridgeview Publishing Co., 1978), p. 10.

13 In this regard see Abiola Irele, *In Praise of Alienation*, an inaugural lecture delivered on November 22, 1982, at the University of Ibadan (Published by Abiola Irele, 1987), *passim.* It is interesting to note, however, that Irele fails to capitalize on the negative value of alienation when he is concerned with the contemporary developments of African philosophy. In this regard see his substantial introduction to Paulin J. Hountondji's book, *African Philosophy: Myth and Reality* (Bloomington: Indiana University Press, 1983), *passim.*

14 Hans-Georg Gadamer, *Philosophical Apprenticeships* (Cambridge, Mass.: MIT Press, 1985), p. 177. Gadamer is here defending himself against those who have reduced hermeneutics to a fad and use this fad either to hide methodological sterility or as a justification for the absence of method. Even if such a defense is justified, it is ironic that Gadamer—who claims that philosophy is hermeneutical in its very nature—should take offense and react so strongly to the "popular" acclaim of his basic and productive insight. As I hope the reader will see, my use of Gadamer is not "faddish" but concretely grounded in the nature of the questions with which I am concerned.

15 Ernest Wamba-Dia-Wamba, "Philosophy in Africa: Challenges of the African Philosopher," in *African Philosophy: The Essential Readings*, ed. Tsenay Serequeberhan (New York: Paragon House, 1991), p. 230. As Wamba puts: "Why, indeed, are hermeneutics, phenomenology, Althusserianism, logical positivism, Hegelianism, structuralism, pragmatism, dialectical materialism, Thomism, etc., all products of specific material and symbolic conditions (specific ideological struggles), understood by our African philosophers as so many correct responses to the philosophical question in Africa?" (ibid.). All I would like to say at this point is that Wamba's question has a boomerang effect on his own "Africanized" Marxist-Leninist position, which he does not address. To be sure, the question is to the point and, as I shall show in this chapter, can be adequately engaged—in all its cultural and historico-political richness—only from an Africanist hermeneutic perspective radically and critically informed by and absorbed in its own lived historicalness.

16 V. Y. Mudimbe, "African Gnosis: Philosophy and the Order of Knowledge," *African Studies Review*, vol. 28, nos. 2/3 (June/September 1985), pp. 210–11.

17 I derive this distinction from an exploration of Martin Heidegger, *Discourse on Thinking* (New York: Harper & Row, 1966); Hans-Georg Gadamer, *Truth and Method* (New York: Crossroad Publishers, 1982), second part; and Thomas S. Kuhn, *The Structure of Scientific Revolutions*, 2d ed. (Chicago: University of Chicago Pres, 1970), *passim*.

18 In this regard see Martin Heidegger's "Modern Science, Metaphysics, and Mathematics," in *Basic Writings*, ed. David Farrell Krell (New York: Harper & Row, 1977).

19 For the work of these two thinkers, please see *Ethiopian Philosophy*, vol. 2, The Treatise of Zar'a Ya'aqob and Walda Heywat, text and authorship (Addis Abeba: Printed for the Addis Abeba University by Commercial Printing Press, 1976), prepared by Dr. Claude Sumner.

20 Elungu, "La philosophie, condition du developpement en Afrique aujourd'hui," p. 8, my own translation.

21 Okere, *African Philosophy: A Historico-Hermeneutical Investigation*, p. xiv.

22 Martin Heidegger, *Being and Time* (New York: Harper & Row, 1962), division two, section 69, *passim* and specifically p. 416. See also, section 68 and section 73, *passim* and specifically p. 430. For Heidegger, who is the most important figure in contemporary hermeneutics, the term "has been," which appears sporadically in differing forms in the texts indicated and throughout *Being and Time*, designates the past that is felt and makes itself felt in the presence of the present. It is a living past that structures the lived actuality of historical *Dasein*—the concrete historicity

of human existence. As we shall soon see in our further elaboration of this point in this chapter, this is what Gadamer refers to and appropriates as "effective history."

23 I have placed the term "greatness" in quotation marks to indicate that my concern, in using it, is not to praise and extol the "greatness" of ancient Africa but merely to point to the fact that the African past did have moments of greatness embodied in a variety of ancient civilizations, such as Axum, Mali, Soghai, Ghana, and Egypt, with all their contradictions and internal problems. My project is thus not defined by a "Diopian" (to borrow a word from Asante) longing for the "greatness" of ancient Africa, but by a critical and historical engagement with the historicity of the African situation. As the reader will see, the second section of chapter 2 will concretely substantiate this perspective in its critical and destructuring reading of the essentialist *Négritude* of Leopold Sedar Senghor.

24 This is what Gadamer refers to as the "effective-historical consciousness." For a discussion of this term and for a thematic exploration of its origins in Heidegger's Being-question, see my paper, "Heidegger and Gadamer: Thinking as 'Meditative' and as 'Effective-Historical Consciousness,' " *Man and World*, vol. 20, no. 1 (1987).

25 Okonda Okolo, "Tradition and Destiny: Horizons of an African Philosophical Hermeneutics," in *African Philosophy: The Essential Readings*, ed. Tsenay Serequeberhan (New York: Paragon House, 1991), p. 207.

26 Kwasi Wiredu, *Philosophy and An African Culture* (New York: Cambridge University Press, 1980), p. 1; Paulin J. Hountondji, *African Philosophy, Myth and Reality*, p. 67.

27 Heidegger, *Being and Time*, p. 255. In this regard see also, "Letter on Humanism," in *Basic Writings*, ed. David Farrell Krell (New York: Harper & Row, 1977), p. 209.

28 Ibid., p. 67

29 For an overview of the discussions provoked by Heidegger's Nazism brought about by Victor Farias's book, *Heidegger and Nazism* (Philadelphia: Temple University Press, 1989), see Kathleen Wright, "The Heidegger Controversy—Updated and Appraised," *Praxis International*, vol. 13, no. 1 (April 1993). For a concise and revealing discussion of this scandalous affair, see, Thomas Sheehan, "Heidegger and the Nazis," in *The New York Review of Books*, vol. 35, no. 10 (June 16, 1988). For a variety of views on this question by Gadamer, Habermas, Derrida, Blanchot, Lacoue-Labarthe, and Levinas, all contemporary European philosophers whose work has been critically influenced by Heidegger's Being-question, see *Critical Inquiry*, vol. 15, no. 2 (Winter 1989), "Symposium on Heidegger and Nazism," ed. Arnold I. Davidson. In this regard it is imperative to remember the words of Aimé Césaire, the Martiniquian poet and philosopher of *Négritude* (a *Négritude* fundamentally at odds with Senghor's essentialism of "Negro-ness"). On this point Césaire writes: "Yes, it would be worthwhile to study clinically, in detail, the steps taken by Hitler and Hitlerism and to reveal to the very distinguished, very humanistic, very Christian bourgeois of the twentieth century that without his being aware of it, he has a Hitler inside him, that Hitler *inhabits* him, that Hitler is his *demon*, that if he rails against him, he is being inconsistent and that, at bottom, what he cannot forgive Hitler for is not *crime* in itself, *the crime against man*, it is not *the humiliation of man as such*, it is the crime against the white

man, the humiliation of the white man, and the fact that he applied to Europe colonialist procedures which until then had been reserved exclusively for the Arabs of Algeria, the coolies of India, and the blacks of Africa [and, we might add, the exterminated aboriginal populations of Australia, North and South America, and more recently the Palestinian Arabs, at the hands of the victimizing victims of the Holocaust]." *Discourse on Colonialism*, originally published in French in 1955 (New York: Monthly Review Press, 1972), p. 14. Needless to say, not one of the above thinkers—who appropriately lament and condemn Heidegger's Nazi connection—least of all Jürgen Habermas, the "philosopher of modernity" (the age of "imperialist colonialism," to borrow Lenin's phrase), has made racism, colonialism, or the expansionist aggressive nature of European modernity a problem for his thought or the focus of his reflections. This silence, this un-said, might just be the "demon" that needs to be exorcised. But under what "banner" is this exorcism to be performed? Who is to be the exorciser?

30   Martin Heidegger, *Being and Time*, p. 377. As the translators, J. Macquarrie and E. Robinson explain: "The root-meaning of the word 'ecstasis' (Greek εκστασισ; German, *Ekstase*) is 'standing outside'. Used generally in Greek for the 'removal' or 'displacement' of something, it came to be applied to states-of-mind which we would now call 'ecstatic'. Heidegger usually keeps the basic root-meaning in mind, but he also is keenly aware of its close connection with the root-meaning of the word 'existence' " (p. 377, note 2). This affinity of the terms "ecstatic" and "existence" is central not only for *Being and Time* but for Heidegger's work as a whole. In "Letter on Humanism" and throughout his later works the term "existence" is rendered as "ek-sistence" in order to accentuate this affinity and to suggest that human existence is the process of its own ecstatic going beyond—hence "standing outside"—itself. The human being is the *Da*—the "there" or openness—of Being which is interior to Being itself. In other words, Heidegger is not merely rejecting humanism out of hand; rather, he is thinking a nonmetaphysical humanism grounded on the *Da*'s interiority to Being. Throughout this chapter and the study as a whole, the reader is advised to keep in mind the above key interpretation of the term "existence" as "ek-sistence." Finally, on p. 205 of the "Letter on Humanism," Heidegger writes that the statement: "The 'essence' of *Dasein* lies in its existence," does not "contain a universal statement about *Dasein*, since the word came into fashion in the eighteenth century as a name for 'object', intending to express the metaphysical concept of the actuality of the actual." As the careful reader can easily ascertain, this refers to the term *Dasein* and its origins and not to the existentiality of human existence which it indicates.

31   Heidegger himself suggests this point in his discussions with a Japanese philosopher in, *On the Way to Language*, (New York: Harper & Row, 1982). See the first section titled, "A Dialogue on Language," *passim*. In his already cited book, Theophilus Okere also notes this point. However, in his explication he unduly restricts this fecund suggestion. In this regard see *African Philosophy: A Historico-Hermeneutical Investigation*, pp. 118–19.

32   In this regard, see Heidegger's last statement of his views, "Modern Natural Science and Technology," in *Radical Phenomenology*, ed. J. Sallis (Atlantic Highlands, N.J.: Humanities Press, 1978), p. 4. For Heidegger's overall perspective on technology and the situation of the modern world, see *The Question concerning Technology and Other Essays*, trans. William Lovitt (New York: Harper & Row, 1977). For

the sense of the term *Ge-stell* and its English rendering as "enframing," see Lovitt's introduction to the text, p. xxix, and in the text, see p. 19.

33 Wamba, "Philosophy in Africa: Challenges of the African Philosopher," *African Philosophy: The Essential Readings*, p. 239.

34 Heidegger, *Being and Time*, p. 346.

35 Basil Davidson, *Africa in Modern History* (New York: Penguin Books, 1985), p. 44.

36 Antonio Gramsci, *Quaderni Del Carcere*, vol. 2, edizione critica dell'Instituto Gramsci, a cura di Valentino Gerratana (Torino: Giulio Einaudi, 1975), pp. 1376–77, my own translation.

37 Ibid., p. 1378, my own translation.

38 For a classic description of this momentous moment in the self-institution of modernity and the destruction of the non-European world which justifies and welcomes it as the objective self-unfolding of *Weltgeist*, see Karl Marx and Frederick Engels, *The Communist Manifesto* (New York: International Publishers, 1983), pp. 10–13.

39 Okolo, "Tradition and Destiny: Horizons of an African Philosophical Hermeneutics," in *African Philosophy: The Essential Readings*, p. 201.

40 Ibid.

41 In this regard, see Martin Heidegger, *Discourse on Thinking* (New York: Harper & Row, 1966), the second part, "Conversation on a Country Path about Thinking," *passim*.

42 Okolo, "Tradition and Destiny," p. 204.

43 Martin Heidegger, *An Introduction to Metaphysics* (New Haven, Conn.: Yale University Press, 1977), p. 176.

44 Ibid.

45 Okolo, "Tradition and Destiny," p. 203.

46 Gadamer, *Truth and Method*, p. 325, and pp. 273–74.

47 Hans-Georg Gadamer, *Reason in the Age of Science* (Cambridge, Mass.: MIT Press, 1981), pp. 109–10. In this regard see also my already cited paper, "Heidegger and Gadamer: Thinking as 'Meditative' and as 'Effective–Historical Consciousness,' " p. 56 and pp. 59–60. For an interesting discussion of this point centered on the Habermas-Gadamer debate and on Vico's notion of "*sensus communis*," see John D. Schaefer, *Sensus Communis* (Durham, N.C.: Duke University Press, 1990), pp. 117–22. I would like to thank Nuhad Jamal for this last reference.

48 Drew Hyland, *The Origins of Philosophy* (New York: Capricorn Books, 1973), p. 289; and by the same author, *The Virtue of Philosophy* (Athens: Ohio University Press, 1981), pp. 12–13. This is a central problem of Heidegger's thought located in the ontic-ontological ambiguity of his ontological analysis and its ontic specificity, or lack thereof, in relation to particular political and historical questions. I cannot here consider, at great length, this important concern except to say that the specific way in which African hermeneutics is here being articulated and the distinctive history out of which it emerges precludes the dangers inherent in Heidegger's position. This is so precisely because the hermeneutical orientation of African

philosophy is firmly wedded to an emancipatory political *praxis* and an ontic historical orientation aimed at the recognition and celebration of cultural-historical variety and difference.

49   Gadamer, *Truth and Method*, pp. 267–68. For the source of Gadamer's conception of "effective-history," see Heidegger, *Being and Time*, division two, part five, section 73, p. 430.

50   Okolo, "Tradition and Destiny," p. 208. See also, S. K. Dabo, "Negro-African Nationalism as a Quest for Justice," *Presence Africaine*, no. 107, 3d quarterly (1978), *passim*.

51   Okolo, ibid., p. 205.

52   Amilcar Cabral, "Anonymous Soldiers for the United Nations," in *Revolution in Guinea: Selected Texts* (New York: Monthly Review Press, 1969), pp. 50–52. In view of what has been said in note 7, it should be noted that the United Nations just as any other complex body that encompasses within itself conflicting and contending forces around formal principles and norms of behavior is a site of struggle and hegemonic contention. In this regard, what Cabral is affirming is an achievement that is sanctioned by the formal principles of the United Nations and yet has been secured against the interests of the dominant forces within it, i.e., the United States and its NATO allies. For an interesting discussion of the "functioning" of the United Nations in terms of "its" most recent international crisis, the colonial legacy of the non-European world, and in the context of superpower reconciliation, see, Erskine B. Childers, "The Use and Abuse of the UN in the Gulf Crisis," *Middle East Report*, no. 169, vol. 21, no. 2 (March/April 1991). For a detailed exposition of the United Nation's partiality in its selective application of international norms and standards, see Norman Finkelstein, "Israel and Iraq: A Double Standard," *Journal of Palestine Studies*, vol. 20, no. 2 (Winter 1991).

53   Cabral, ibid., pp. 51–52.

54   See note 44.

55   See note 44. From within the concrete situation of the Eritrean anti-colonial struggle Issayas Afewerki expresses this view in the following manner: "the attainment of the objectives of our national cause—independence and liberation from Ethiopian colonial rule—take precedence over other issues, and because of various other regional considerations, we have chosen to avoid involvement in any regional conflicts or inter-Arab disputes. We have chosen to concentrate our efforts on our main objective, which is victory over Ethiopian colonial rule." *Foreign Broadcast Information Service*, Daily Report, Sub-Saharan Africa, Thursday 12 July 1990, p. 8.

56   For the relevant quotation in full and reference please see, in this chapter, note 48.

57   Fanon, *Black Skins, White Masks*, p. 229. The character of this historically grounded and oriented inventiveness—that invents out of its "has been" its as-of-yet unrealized original future possibilities—will be the main concern of chapter 4.

58   Cheikh Hamidou Kane, *Ambiguous Adventure* (Portsmouth N.H.: Heinemann Educational Books, 1989), pp. 79–80, emphasis added. On this point, see also, Lucius Outlaw, "African 'Philosophy': Deconstructive and Reconstructive Challenges," in *Contemporary Philosophy: A New Survey*, vol. 5, African Philosophy,

ed. Guttorm Floistad (Dordrecht, Netherlands: Martinus Nijhoff, 1987), pp. 35–36.

59 Fanon, *The Wretched of the Earth*, p. 311.

60 *The Portable Nietzsche*, trans. Walter Kaufmann (New York: Viking Press, 1974), p. 125. I would like to thank Robert Gooding-Williams for helping me locate this reference.

61 Amilcar Cabral, *Revolution in Guinea: Selected Texts*, p. 76.

62 Fanon, *The Wretched of the Earth*, p. 233. It is important to note, as is clear from the context, that Fanon's remarks—which I have slightly modified in quoting—refer in the singular to all the differing historico-cultural totalities that in sum constitute the cultural and historical actuality of the continent in all its diversity and difference.

63 Aimé Césaire, "Letter to Maurice Thorez," English translation, *Presence Africaine* (Paris: Presence Africaine, 1957), pp. 6–7.

64 Okolo, "Tradition and Destiny," p. 209.

65 Ibid., p. 202.

66 For an extremely condensed synopsis of this perspective see my paper, "The African Liberation Struggle: A Hermeneutic Exploration of an African Historical-Political Horizon," *Ultimate Reality and Meaning*, Interdisciplinary Studies in the Philosophy of Understanding (Canadian Journal), vol. 14, no. 1 (March 1991).

67 Heidegger, *Being and Time*, p. 358. Regarding presuppositions and the educational and lived background or context in which and out of which one philosophizes, Kwasi Wiredu writes: "Suppose now that a critic should attribute what I have written to my particular educational background; I am bound to concede as much. In a certain obvious sense we are all children of our circumstances. But were the existence of such a 'bias' proof of falsity, universal silence would be obligatory on all mankind" (*Philosophy and an African Culture*, p. 36). On the same crucial point Ernest Wamba-Dia-Wamba observes that: "The paradox in philosophy is that the selection of a conception or the definition of philosophy one makes is necessarily an expression of one's philosophical position, stand, and outlook." "Philosophy in Africa: Challenges of the African Philosopher," in *African Philosophy: The Essential Readings*, p. 236. In both of these remarks (remarks by contemporary African philosophers) there is a failure to recognize the hermeneutical truth that the lived situatedness of philosophy is not a blemish but the source of philosophical reflection as such. In fact one needs to begin from the recognition that philosophy is "its own time apprehended in thoughts," as Hegel puts it in the preface to the *Philosophy of Right*, trans. T. M. Knox (Oxford University Press, 1973), p. 11. Once this point is grasped the "fear" of "bias" and "paradox" is dissipated and the hermeneutically circular character of philosophy and its practice, grounded on "*Dasein*'s circular Being" (Heidegger, *Being and Time*, p. 363), can properly be seen as the fecund origin of philosophy itself. In this regard, see Theophilus Okere's already cited book, *African Philosophy: A Historico-Hermeneutical Investigation*, chap. five. See also, Lucius Outlaw, "African and African-American Philosophy: Deconstruction and the Critical Management of Traditions," in *The Journal*, vol. 1, no. 1 (Winter–Spring 1984).

2. African Philosophy

All emphasis in the original unless otherwise indicated.

1 For an interesting, if understated, documentation of the political conflicts and war expenditures of this period of "world peace" for Africa, see "What Price the African Soldier?" *Africa Now*, no. 15 (July 1982), *passim*, and specifically p. 22; author not given.

2 For a concise discussion of Portuguese colonialism as a European-North American phenomenon, see Jay O'Brien, "Portugal in Africa," *Monthly Review Press*, vol. 26 (May 1974); see also Richard Gibson, *African Liberation Movements* (New York: Oxford University Press, 1972), part five; and Basil Davidson, *The Liberation of Guinea* (Baltimore: Penguin Books, 1969), *passim*.

3 In other words, beyond European colonialism, one has to recognize the question of the former Spanish-Sahara and Eritrea as cases of African colonialism by Morocco and Ethiopia, respectively. On the other hand, the Ogaden, Oromia, and South Sudan are also in a semi-colonial relationship to the dominant ethnic group(s) which control the particular geographic area(s) these people inhabit. In spite of their differences all these situations are cases of external occupation of an ethnic or national territory. For a similar view on this point, see Basil Davidson's preface to Richard Sherman's *Eritrea: The Unfinished Revolution* (New York: Praeger, 1980).

4 The paradigmatic example of this is the Horn of Africa, where the Ethiopian government of Mengistu Hailemariam (1974–1991) for seventeen years used famine as a weapon of war not only against the colonized people of Eritrea but also against its own citizens in Tigray and Wollo.

5 By the term "African peoples" I mean to refer to the inhabitants of the continent as a whole minus the Whites of South Africa. I use the term collectively, moreover, not in order to level off the variety and multiplicity that constitutes the inhabitants of the continent, nor to establish some "true" African "Essence" *à la* Senghor, but rather to highlight the common experience of European colonialism and neocolonialism that, since the last quarter of the nineteenth century, has imposed on the inhabitants of the continent a shared destiny or a sense of historical place in the antagonistic context of a European dominated world. I exclude the Whites of South Africa precisely because they see themselves as distinct and apart—Apartheid—from the rest of the continent in this specific particular.

6 By the term "problematic" I mean a group of texts centered around an internally interconnected cluster of concerns engaged in exploring a theme which conversely defines and governs the questions and answers that are possible from within the confines of said "problematic." The communist philosopher Louis Althusser inaugurates the term in *For Marx*, trans. Ben Brewster (New York: Pantheon Books, 1969), pp. 55–71, specifically p. 66 and p. 253. To be sure, the use and appropriation of this term does not in any way implicate me in Althusser's reading of Marx from which it is derived. For an interesting comment on and appropriation of Althusser's concept of "problematic" see, Edward W. Said, *Orientalism* (New York: Vintage Books, 1979), p. 16. The use I make of this term is also akin to Thomas S. Kuhn's concept of "paradigm," as established in *The Structure of Scientific Revolutions*, 2d ed. (Chicago: University of Chicago Press, 1970). In like manner Martin Heidegger's

notion of "dis-closure" is centered around the idea that texts and discourses are hatched out of an originative ground of problems and concerns which is then constituted and established in these texts and discourses. For a discussion of the similitude in Kuhn and Heidegger, on this point, see my already cited paper, "Heidegger and Gadamer: Thinking as 'Meditative' and as 'Effective-Historical Consciousness,'" p. 43.

7 Theophilus Okere, *African Philosophy: A Historico-Hermeneutical Investigation of the Conditions of Its Possibility* (Lanham, Md.: University Press of America, 1983), p. 121.

8 I do not intend to present an extensive discussion of every ideological position that could be located in the discourse on the African liberation struggle. I therefore restrict myself to these two personalities, precisely because their ideological positions enclose—from contrary points—the literature of the African liberation struggle as a whole. One more point: Throughout this study, in connection with Senghor, I will use and show a preference for the term *Africanité* as opposed to *Négritude* precisely because, for Senghor, this is the more inclusive and appropriate term, as a designation of his work and ideological position. On this point, see Leopold Sedar Senghor, *The Foundations of "Africanité" or "Négritude" and "Arabité"* (Paris: Presence Africaine, 1971), pp. 7, 39, and 61. In contradistinction to the above, the term *Négritude* will be reserved and used in connection with Aimé Césaire's work.

9 Kwame Nkrumah, *Towards Colonial Freedom* (London: Panaf Books, 1979). It is interesting to note that this pamphlet ends with the slogan: "Colonial and Subject Peoples of the World—Unite!" (ibid., p. 45). This is the concluding slogan of the *Communist Manifesto* properly adjusted, at least on the level of verbiage, to the African colonial situation.

10 Kwame Nkrumah, *Class Struggle in Africa* (New York: International Publishers, 1975), pp. 51 and 53. For an interesting discussion of Nkrumah's Marxism-Leninism, see Ali A. Mazrui, "Borrowed Theory and Original Practice in African Politics," in *Patterns of African Development: Five Comparisons*, ed. Herbert J. Spiro (Englewood Cliffs, N.J.: Prentice-Hall, 1967), pp. 105–17.

11 Nkrumah, *Class Struggle in Africa*, pp. 52–53.

12 To be sure, this is an existential and hermeneutical truth of our lived facticity that philosophic thought neglects at its own peril. In this regard see also Gerard Chaliand's interesting but more conventional and limited remarks on this point: *Revolutions in the Third World* (New York: Viking Press, 1977), part two, section six. Antonio Gramsci makes this same point in his remarks on Kant and the project of the Enlightenment, in *Antonio Gramsci Quaderni Del Carcere*, vol. 2, ed. Valentino Gerratana (Torino: Gulio Einaudi, 1975), pp. 1484–85.

13 In this regard, see Aimé Césaire's historic 1956 *Letter to Thorez*, trans. Presence Africaine (Paris: Presence Africaine, 1957), *passim*, and the politico-philosophic orientation represented by Fanon and Cabral.

14 Aimé Césaire, *Discourse on Colonialism* (New York: Monthly Review Press, 1972), pp. 78–79.

15 Martin Heidegger, *An Introduction to Metaphysics* (New Haven and London: Yale University Press, 1977), p. 152.

16 *The Marx-Engels Reader*, ed. Robert C. Tucker, see "Contribution to the Critique of Hegel's *Philosophy of Right*: Introduction" (New York: W. W. Norton & Co., 1978), p. 65.

17 In other words, the politics of African liberation cannot presuppose an already established historical and philosophical ground. In fact, on the level of theory, this is precisely what the struggle aims to achieve and thus cannot simply presuppose it without neglecting its very *raison d'être*.

18 Within the context of the African liberation struggle I am suggesting that we need to take seriously the problematic of historicity and the hermeneuticity of human existence if we are to grasp the originative and world-founding character of the African struggle for freedom. In this regard, see Martin Heidegger, *Being and Time* (New York: Harper & Row, 1962), division two, section five.

19 Paulin J. Hountondji, *African Philosophy, Myth and Reality* (Bloomington: Indiana University Press, 1983), pp. 135–37.

20 Ibid., p. 136. In chapter 3 of *Consciencism* Nkrumah attempts to indicate the specific African orientation of his work.

21 Ibid., pp. 141–42.

22 On this point, see Martin Heidegger, *The Question concerning Technology and Other Essays*, trans. William Lovitt (New York: Harper & Row, 1977).

23 What we have done thus far is to merely problematize the Marxist-Leninist perspective in terms of the concrete context of the African situation. For the larger framework out of which this critique is developed, see Kostas Axelos, *Alienation, Praxis, & Techne in the Thought of Karl Marx* (University of Texas Press, 1976); Cornelius Castoriadis, *The Imaginary Institution of Society* (Cambridge, Mass.: MIT Press, 1987), part 1; and by the same author, *Crossroads in the Labyrinth*, the section titled, "Value, Equality, Justice, Politics: From Marx to Aristotle and from Aristotle to Ourselves" (Cambridge, Mass.: MIT Press, 1984), pp. 260–330.

24 Hountondji, *African Philosophy*, p. 160.

25 Ibid., part one, sections 1, 2, and 3. According to Hountondji Temples's work does not qualify as African philosophy precisely because Temples is not an African. This is the depth of Hountondji's insight in formulating his "geographic" conception of African philosophy.

26 Kwame Nkrumah, " 'African Socialism' Revisited" (1966), collected in *Revolutionary Path*, a Panaf select anthology of Nkrumah's work (London: Panaf Books, 1980), p. 444.

27 Nkrumah, *Class Struggle in Africa*, p. 25.

28 " 'African Socialism' Revisited" (1966) and "The Myth of the 'Third World' " (1968), in *Revolutionary Path*, *passim*.

29 Ibid., "The Myth of the 'Third World,' " p. 438.

30 Ibid., " 'African Socialism' Revisited," pp. 444–45. For Hountondji's explicit endorsement of this text, see *African Philosophy, Myth and Reality*, p. 137.

31 In this respect, see F. Engels, *Socialism: Utopian and Scientific*, and *The Dialectics of Nature*, in which Marx's thought, from a critical perspective on and a critique

of capitalist society, is transformed into an encyclopedic compendium of wisdom and "objective" truth.

32 Leopold Sedar Senghor, *Prose and Poetry*, trans. John Reed and Clive Wake (London: Heinemann Educational Books, 1976), p. 33.

33 The classic texts in this regard are Marx's writings from the *Grundrisse* which have been published separately under the title, *Pre-Capitalist Economic Formations*, introduced by E. J. Hobsbawm (New York: International Publishers, 1975), and the two central works written in conjunction with Engels: *The German Ideology* (1845), and *The Communist Manifesto* (1848), along with the famous biographical preface to *A Contribution to the Critique of Political Economy* (1859). For an interesting critique of Marx's position, see Claude Lefort, *The Political Forms of Modern Society* (Cambridge, Mass.: MIT Press, 1986), part two, section five, *passim*, and by the same author, *Democracy and Political Theory*, (Minneapolis: University of Minnesota Press, 1988), part two, section eight, *passim*.

34 In this regard, see Leopold Sedar Senghor, *The Foundations of "Africanité" or "Négritude" and "Arabité,"* trans. Mercer Cook (Paris: Presence Africaine, 1971), *passim*.

35 Leopold Sedar Senghor, "Constructive Elements of a Civilization of African Negro Inspiration," in *Presence Africaine*, nos. 24–25 (February–May 1959), p. 290. It should be noted that, two years earlier (1957), the only Black African country to have gained independence was the Gold Coast, which was renamed Ghana under the leadership of Kwame Nkrumah.

36 Ibid., p. 291.

37 Leopold Sedar Senghor, "The Spirit of Civilization or the Laws of African Negro Culture," in *Presence Africaine*, nos. 8–10 (June–November 1956), p. 52.

38 Ibid., p. 52.

39 Ibid., p. 59.

40 Ibid., p. 58.

41 Ibid., p. 64.

42 Ibid.

43 For a concise presentation of Lucien Levy-Bruhl's views, please see L. A. Claire's introduction to *Primitive Mentality* (Boston: Beacon Press, 1966).

44 Senghor, "Constructive Elements of a Civilization of African Negro Inspiration" (1959), p. 268.

45 Indeed, as is well known, for Hegel in the *Phenomenology*, the arduous labor of consciousness is aimed at elevating itself to the level of self-conscious freedom, i.e., human/spiritual existence in contradistinction to its initial and unfree—nonhuman—*natural* determination. Indeed as Hegel categorically affirms in paragraph no. 187, human existence—which is self-conscious freedom—is not "natural" but is gained at the risk of natural existence. This is the significance of Hegel's master-slave dialectic. On the social-historical level this is also the process by which human existence is established. In the *Philosophy of Right* (paragraph 141 and remarks), this is the level at which the moral consciousness or "morality" is sublated and emerges anew as "ethical life" which, for Hegel, is the true human community.

46   Leopold Sedar Senghor, "Latinity and Négritude," in *Presence Africaine*, vol. 24, no. 52, fourth quarterly (1964), p. 14. On this point, see also Edward W. Said, *Orientalism* (New York: Vintage Books, 1979), p. 206. It is interesting to note how Senghor's clear distinction between "art" and "science"—Africa and Europe—fits flawlessly the traditional European metaphysical distinction on this point, first articulated by Plato in book X of the *Republic*. For Plato, however, the superiority of "science" and the inferiority of "art," was itself the normative ground of this distinction. In effect, this is true for Senghor as well, even if it is unwittingly that he gets implicated in this rather derogatory self-conception. Senghor's "learned" submissiveness to this position might even be the mark of his personal inferiority, which he "generously" claims for all of us.

47   Leopold Sedar Senghor, "Négritude: A Humanism of the Twentieth Century," in *The African Reader: Independent Africa*, ed. Wilfred Cartey and Martin Kilson (New York: Random House, 1970), p. 180.

48   Said, *Orientalism*, pp. 67–72, and 73.

49   For Senghor, the Negro-African and Arab-Berber is, ethnographically and essentially speaking, a "Fluctuant," a being determined in its essence by emotion. On this point, see Senghor, *The Foundations of Africanité*, pp. 37–45 and *passim*. As Said points out this is the basic perspective of the Orientalist. See *Orientalism*, pp. 40, 70, and 273.

50   Frantz Fanon, *Black Skin, White Masks* (New York: Grove Press, 1967), *passim*. In this regard it is important to note that in "Orientalism Revisited" (*Cultural Critique*, vol. 1 [Fall 1985]), Said acknowledges Fanon's and Césaire's strong influence on his own work.

51   Said, *Orientalism*, pp. 45–46.

52   Georg Wilhelm Friedrich Hegel, *The Philosophy of History*, introduced by C. J. Friedrich (New York: Dover Publications, 1956), pp. 91–99.

53   Frantz Fanon, *Towards the African Revolution* (New York: Grove Press, 1988), p. 44. This quotation is taken from the essay, "Racism and Culture," which originally was Fanon's contribution to the First Congress of Negro-African Writers and Artists, held in Paris in 1956. At this same congress Senghor read his paper, "The Spirit of Civilization or the Laws of African Negro Culture," from which I have already cited extensively.

54   Said, *Orientalism*, p. 277. Indeed, *Africanité* is, for Senghor, not the empirical enumeration of characteristics but the essential constitution of what it means to be a Negro.

55   As quoted by Said, ibid., p. 97. See also Said, pp. 221–25.

56   Ibid., p. 108.

57   Ibid.

58   Senghor, *The Foundations of "Africanité,"* p. 15.

59   Ibid., p. 83.

60   Leopold Sedar Senghor, *On African Socialism*, trans. Mercer Cook (New York: Praeger, 1964), p. 75, emphasis added.

61   Ibid., p. 165.

62 Ibid., p. 70.

63 Ibid., p. 72.

64 Ibid., p. 74.

65 Ibid., p. 12; and see also pp. 136–37.

66 Senghor quotes these lines: "those who never invented anything . . . who never explored anything . . . who never tamed anything" [but who abandon themselves] "to the essence of all things"—and gives them his own essentialist reading ("Constructive Elements of a Civilization of African Negro Inspiration," *Presence Africaine*, nos. 24–25 [February–May 1959], p. 267). It should be noted that Aimé Césaire, the author of these lines, does not subscribe to Senghor's reading. In this regard see Césaire's 1967 interview with Rene Depestre, in *Discourse on Colonialism* (New York: Monthly Review Press, 1972), pp. 65–79; and Clayton Eshleman's and Annette Smith's introduction to *Aimé Césaire: The Collected Poetry* (Berkeley: University of California Press, 1983), pp. 1–28.

67 On this point see, in this chapter, my earlier discussion of Hegel. In *Ambiguous Adventure* Cheikh Hamidou Kane must have had Senghor's duplicitous *Africanité* in mind when he has his main character, Samba Diallo, say: "It is not in a difference of nature between the West and what is not the West that I should see the explanation of the opposition in their destinies. If there were a difference of nature, it would follow in effect that if the West is right, and speaks in a loud voice, what is not the West is necessarily wrong and ought to be silent; that if the West moves beyond its borders and colonizes, this situation is in the nature of things and is definitive" (ibid., pp. 151–52).

68 Okonda Okolo, "Tradition and Destiny: Horizons of an African Philosophical Hermeneutics," in *African Philosophy: The Essential Readings*, ed. Tsenay Serequeberhan (Paragon, 1991), p. 201.

69 In this respect the most important novel (and film) is Ousmane Sembene's *Xala*, trans. Clive Wake (Chicago, Ill.: Lawrence Hill Books, 1976).

70 I have "opposite extremes" in double quotation marks because for the neocolonized African whether the regime in power is affiliated with the Western (Senghor) or Eastern (Nkrumah) Bloc is—in real terms—completely immaterial. What differs, in each case, is the ideological justification and sugar coating. The effect, in either case is the same, i.e., the nonhistoricity of African existence. Two good examples of this are Moi's Kenya and Mengistu's Ethiopia. In Kenya the regime maintains itself in power by terrorizing and marginalizing the citizenry. In Ethiopia this state of affairs came to an abrupt end in mid-1991, with the Ethiopian people forcefully reclaiming their right to historical existence.

71 Count Yorck, as quoted by Heidegger, in *Being and Time*, p. 452.

3. Colonialism and the Colonized

All emphasis in the original unless otherwise indicated.

1 Kwasi Wiredu, "The Question of Violence in Contemporary African Political Thought," *Praxis International*, vol. 6, no. 3 (October 1986); and Henry Odera Oruka, *Punishment and Terrorism in Africa* (Nairobi, Kenya: East African Literature Bureau, 1976).

2   As Jean-Paul Sartre has observed, since Sorel, Fanon is the one thinker who has seriously engaged and examined the internal dialectic of violence and counter-violence, in the specific context of an oppressive setup. (See the preface to *The Wretched of the Earth* [New York: Grove Press, 1968], p. 14.) In this respect, Kenneth David Kaunda's book, *The Riddle of Violence* (New York: Harper & Row, 1980), is not useful for our present discussion, precisely because it is not a systemic study of a violent setup, but the conscientious musings of a Christian nonviolent politician in the face of the all-pervasive presence of violence in politics.

3   Aimé Césaire, *Discourse on Colonialism* (New York: Monthly Review Press, 1972), p. 9. In this respect see also Cornelius Castoriadis, "The Crises of Western Societies," *Telos*, no. 53 (Fall 1982), pp. 26–28. In "Defending the West," *Partisan Review*, no. 3 (1984), Castoriadis argues that South Africa cannot be considered part of the Western world because it violates the basic premises of the European heritage. He fails to note, however, that the West as a whole is responsible for the present existence of South Africa and furthermore, the West has never acted in accordance with its heritage (i.e., its self-conception) in its relations with non-European peoples.

4   Césaire, ibid., p. 11.

5   Edward Said, *The Question of Palestine* (New York: Vintage Books, 1980), p. 78. For a similar description of the colonial experience in its dehumanization of the colonized see Fanon, *The Wretched of the Earth*, p. 250.

6   Karl Marx and Frederick Engels, *The Communist Manifesto* (New York: International Publishers, 1983), pp. 9–13. The relevant passages are: "The discovery of America, the rounding of the Cape, opened up fresh ground [sic] for the rising bourgeoisie. The East Indian and Chinese markets, the colonization of America, trade with the colonies, the increase in the means of exchange and in commodities generally, gave to commerce, to navigation, to industry, an impulse never before known" (pp. 9–10). In other words: "Modern industry has established the world market, for which the discovery [i.e., the colonization] of America paved the way. This market has given an immense development to commerce, to navigation, to communication" (p. 10). Thus: "In a word, it [i.e., the European bourgeoisie] creates a world after its own image" (p. 13). In everything that the bourgeoisie does to globalize Europe it is the "tool of History" and it has Marx's unconditional support. In other words, in the above passages Marx, like a good colonialist, is celebrating the globalization of European temporality. This is the temporality grounded on, as Said tells us, "the conversion into productivity" of the human and natural resources of the non-European world (see note 5).

7   On the theme of colonial fascism see, Albert Memmi, *The Colonizer and the Colonized* (Boston: Beacon Press, 1967), p. 55, and also pp. 62–65. On this point see also—in this study, chapter 1 note 29—Aimé Césaire's already cited insightful remarks on Hitler and Hitlerism and Europe's hypocritical stance toward colonial fascism.

8   Memmi, ibid., p. 3.

9   V. Y. Mudimbe, "African Gnosis: Philosophy and the Order of Knowledge," *African Studies Review*, vol. 28, nos. 2–3 (June–September 1985), p. 154.

10   V. Y. Mudimbe, *The Invention of Africa* (Bloomington: Indiana University Press, 1988), pp. 47–48.

11 T. S. Eliot, *A Choice of Kipling's Verse* (New York: Anchor Books, 1962), p. 143.

12 It should be noted that, to this day, the language of economic "development" and political "maturity" or lack thereof, with which United Nations and World Food experts assess the economic and political situation of non-European territories is internal to this colonialist conception of human existence.

13 Karl Marx, "British Rule in India," in Karl Marx and Frederick Engels, *On Colonialism* (New York: International Publishers, 1972), p. 41.

14 For a detailed exposition of the colonialist orientation of Marx's "materialist conception of history" see my paper, "Karl Marx and African Emancipatory Thought: A Critique of Marx's Euro-Centric Metaphysics," *Praxis International*, vol. 10, nos. 1/2 (April/July 1990).

15 *Hegel's Philosophy of Right*, trans. T. M. Knox (New York: Oxford University Press, 1973), p. 151, paragraph no. 246, emphasis added.

16 Ibid., pp. 151–52, paragraphs no. 246–49.

17 For a detailed discussion of the colonialist orientation of Hegel's thought please see my paper, "The Idea of Colonialism In Hegel's *Philosophy of Right*," *International Philosophical Quarterly*, vol. 29, no. 3, issue no. 115 (September 1989).

18 On this point see Loren Eisely, *Darwin's Century* (New York: Anchor Books, 1961), *passim*; Cornel West, *Prophesy Deliverance!* (Philadelphia: Westminster Press, 1982), chap. two, "A Genealogy of Modern Racism"; and Edward W. Said, "Representing the Colonized: Anthropology's Interlocutors," *Critical Inquiry*, vol. 15, no. 2 (Winter 1989).

19 As quoted by Richard H. Popkin, "Hume's Racism," *The Philosophical Forum*, vol. 9, nos. 2–3 (Winter–Spring 1977–1978); for Hume's remarks, see p. 213; for Kant's remarks, see p. 218.

20 Placide Temples, *Bantu Philosophy* (Paris: Presence Africaine, 1969), pp. 171–72.

21 Aristotle, *Politics*, ed. Stephen Everson (New York: Cambridge University Press, 1989), 1260b6–7, p. 20.

22 On this point see H. D. F. Kitto, *The Greeks* (New York: Penguin Books, 1979). See also, Aristotle, *Politics*, 1252b5–9, p. 2.

23 Alan Ryan, "Professor Hegel Goes to Washington," a review of Francis Fukuyama's *The End of History and the Last Man* (New York: Free Press, 1989), in *The New York Review of Books*, vol. 39, no 6, March 26, 1992, p. 10.

24 Edward Said, "The Burdens of Interpretation and the Question of Palestine," *Journal of Palestine Studies*, vol. 16, no. 1, issue 61 (Autumn 1986), pp. 29–30.

25 In the twenty-sixth chapter of *Capital*, vol. 1, Marx explicates in great detail this whole development, which he refers to as "primitive accumulation." As a true nineteenth-century European, however, Marx's concern is much more focused on the economic mechanisms of accumulation and not on the extirpation of aboriginal populations, which is just mentioned in passing.

26 Aimé Césaire, *Letter to Maurice Thorez* (1956), English translation by *Presence Africaine* (Paris: Presence Africaine, 1957), p. 6.

27 Chinua Achebe, *Things Fall Apart* (New York: A Faucett Premier Book, 1959), p. 191.

28 Ibid.

29 Fanon, *Black Skin, White Masks*, p. 12 (New York: Grove Press, 1967).

30 *Hegel's Phenomenology of Spirit*, trans. A. V. Miller (New York: Clarendon Press, 1977), paragraphs 187 and 188.

31 In this regard, as Kwame Anthony Appiah points out (*In My Father's House* [Oxford University Press, 1992], p. 4) the European colonial attitude toward the colonized was not uniform or homogeneous. For example, the French practiced a policy of assimilation the British did not. This, however, does not invalidate my point that the character of Obierika is the spiritual ancestor of the subjugated *évolué* or Westernized African. My point is not that the British and the French had similar policies or results, but that different as their polices might be they both presuppose the cultural, historical, and political subjugation and subservience of the colonized. In this regard then Obierika symbolizes, in Achebe's narrative, that initial moment of humiliation and subordination that is the necessary point of origin for the consciousness of the Westernized African. In other words—whether it was so intended by the colonizer and whether or not it was accepted on these terms by the colonized—the process of Westernization necessarily presupposes the subjugation and deprecation of the indigenous culture and historicity. This is so precisely because, on epistemic grounds, it is the act of surreptitiously privileging, on a metaphysical level, a particular culture and historicity as being coterminous with Being or existence as such.

32 For an interesting but fundamentally different reading of this text, see Rhonda Cobham, "Problems of Gender and History in the Teaching of *Things Fall Apart*," in *Matatu*, no. 7 (1990).

33 Cheikh Hamidou Kane, *Ambiguous Adventure* (Portsmouth, N.H.: Heinemann Educational Books, 1989), pp. 48–49.

34 For this reference see note 5.

35 *Kant on History*, ed. Lewis White Beck (Indianapolis: Bobbs-Merrill Educational Publishing, 1963), p. 3.

36 Frantz Fanon, *Towards the African Revolution* (New York: Grove Press, 1988), pp. 158–59.

37 Patrick Taylor, *The Narrative of Liberation* (Ithaca: Cornell University Press, 1989), p. 74.

38 Henry Louis Gates, Jr., "Critical Fanonism," *Critical Inquiry*, vol. 17, no 3 (Spring 1991), p. 459. Gates's charge against Said rests on projecting the singular situation of minorities in the U.S.A. as the norm in the non-European world as a whole. It should be noted that the historico-political conflicts that engaged and produced the texts of Fanon are, on the whole, the lived actuality in which we—of the non-EuroAmerican world—still find ourselves.

39 Fanon, *The Wretched of the Earth*, p. 38.

40 Ibid., p. 112.

41 Regarding this key notion of colonization as "thingification," see Aimé Césaire, *Discourse on Colonialism* (New York: Monthly Review Press, 1972), p. 21; and Fanon, *The Wretched of the Earth*, pp. 36–37.

42 Ibid., p. 40.

43 This is the contradiction between the state as the embodiment of "ethical life" and the unresolvable contradictions of "civil society," the realm of socio-economic existence. On this point, see my already cited paper, "The Idea of Colonialism in Hegel's *Philosophy of Right.*"

44 Fanon, *The Wretched of the Earth*, p. 36.

45 Ibid., p. 41.

46 Loren Eisely, *Darwin's Century* (New York: Anchor Books, 1961), chap. ten. See also Edward Said, *The Question of Palestine* (New York: Vintage Books, 1980), pp. 56–83.

47 Fanon, *The Wretched of the Earth*, p. 118.

48 Ibid., pp. 152–56.

49 Ibid., p. 51.

50 Ibid., p. 43.

51 Ibid., p. 51, emphasis added.

52 Jean-Jacques Rousseau, *On the Social Contract*, trans. Donald A. Cress and introduced by Peter Gay (Indianapolis: Hackett, 1983), p. 17. The relevant lines read as follows: "Were I to consider only force and the effect that flows from it, I would say that so long as a people is constrained to obey and does obey, it does well. As soon as it can shake off the yoke and does shake it off, it does even better. For by recovering its liberty by means of the same right that stole it, either the populace is justified in getting it back or else those who took it away were not justified in their actions."

53 Fanon, *The Wretched of the Earth*, p. 69, emphasis added.

54 Memmi, *The Colonizer and the Colonized*, p. 92, emphasis added.

55 Oliva Blanchette, *For a Fundamental Social Ethic* (New York: Philosophical Library, 1973), p. 28.

56 Regarding this conception of the human being as a being that constitutes itself in an ongoing manner in the actuality of its life, see notes 27, 28, and 32 in chapter 1 of this study.

57 Fanon, *The Wretched of the Earth*, p. 51.

58 Albert Memmi, *Dominated Man* (Boston: Beacon Press, 1969), in section 4 "The Domestic Servant," p. 178. It is important to note that the condition of utter humiliation and sexual domination that Memmi highlights based on his reflections on the film *The Servant* (by Harold Pinter and Joseph Losey) is a rather accurate representation of the reality of life, especially for female servants, in most African countries. This is particularly true if the master or employer is himself a Westernized African and a member of the neocolonial ruling class, who culturally aspires and "sees" himself as incarnating European culture.

59 Ibid., p. 179.

60 Ibid.

61 Fanon, *The Wretched of the Earth*, pp. 36–37.

62 Hegel, *Phenomenology of Spirit*, p. 10, paragraph no. 18. As is well known, for Hegel *Wirklichkeit* (actuality) is grounded on the adequation of concept and object.

63 Frantz Fanon, *Les damnes de la terre* (Paris: François Maspero, 1974), p. 6.

64 Patrick Taylor, *The Narrative of Liberation*, p. 49. On this point, it is necessary to emphasize that, Taylor's position, if left unqualified, suffers from a naive essentialism which is grounded on reifying and elevating above the historicity of existence the pre-colonial humanity of the colonized.

65 On this point see the upcoming discussion later in this chapter. In *The Wretched of the Earth*, please see pp. 55–59.

66 For an interesting exposition of this point, please see Michael Ryan, *Marxism and Deconstruction* (Baltimore: Johns Hopkins University Press, 1984), p. 6.

67 Martin Heidegger, *An Introduction to Metaphysics* (New Haven: Yale University Press, 1977), p. 62.

68 Ibid., p. 152.

69 Ibid., p. 155, and the additional exploration of this point on pp. 143–65.

70 Taylor, *The Narrative of Liberation*, p. 60.

71 Jean-Paul Sartre, in the preface to *The Wretched of the Earth*, p. 14.

72 Hannah Arendt, *On Violence* (New York: Harcourt Brace Jovanovich, 1970), p. 65.

73 Hannah Arendt, *Between Past and Future* (New York: Penguin Books, 1980), p. 4.

74 In this regard see Edward W. Said, "An Ideology of Difference," *Critical Inquiry*, vol. 12, no. 1 (Autumn 1985), p. 47. To my knowledge the one European philosopher that is not snared by this Eurocentric double standard is Jean-Paul Sartre. On the other hand, one of the most blatant offenders on this score is Albert Camus. On this last point, see Albert Camus, *Resistance, Rebellion and Death* (New York: Vintage Books, 1974), specifically contrast "Letters to a German Friend" and the section titled "Algeria."

75 As V. Y. Mudimbe points out: "Until the 1950s—and I am not certain at all that things have changed today for the general public in the West—Africa is widely perceived and presented as the continent without memory, without past, without history. More precisely, her history is supposed to commence with her contacts with Europe, specifically with the progressive European invasion of the continent that begins at the end of the fifteenth century." *The Surreptitious Speech* (Chicago: University of Chicago Press, 1992), p. xx.

76 It should be noted, as Fanon points out in his article, "Accra: Africa Affirms Its Unity and Defines Its Strategy" (first published in *El Moudjahid*, no. 34, December 24, 1958; presently collected in *Towards the African Revolution*, section 16 [Grove Press, 1988]), that the counterclaim of the colonized has to do with the relation of forces within which the colonizer-colonized confrontation unfolds. It is only when this relation—globally or regionally—tilts against the colonizing power that we here talk of "non-violent decolonization" (p. 155).

77 Frantz Fanon, *A Dying Colonialism* (New York: Grove Press, 1965), p. 78. In her already cited work *On Violence*, Arendt writes that, "if only the practice of violence would make it possible to interrupt automatic processes in the realm of human affairs, the preachers of violence would have won an important point" (p. 30). In point of fact, as Fanon points out, in the quotation just cited, this is precisely the

case in the colonial context. The inertness of submission to colonial tyranny is replaced by the vitality of anti-colonial resistance and revolution.

78 Ironically Albert Camus was one of the "prestigious French intellectuals" (V. Y. Mudimbe, *The Surreptitious Speech*, p. xvii), who in 1947 was sympathetic to and supportive of Alioune Diop's efforts to establish *Presence Africaine*, a solitary African cultural institution in the heart of post-war France.

79 Memmi, *The Colonizer and the Colonized*, p. 3.

80 Amilcar Cabral, *Return to the Source: Selected Speeches* (New York: Monthly Review Press, 1973), p. 79. In *On Violence*, Arendt is of the opinion that the "civil-rights movement . . . was entirely nonviolent" (p. 76). For a detailed discussion which contradicts Arendt's unsubstantiated assertion, see William R. Jones, "Liberation Strategies in Black Theology: Mao, Martin or Malcolm?" *Philosophy Born of Struggle* (Kendal/Hunt Publishing Co., 1983).

81 Fanon, *The Wretched of the Earth*, p. 56.

82 On this point see, Paul Nizan's interesting short novel, *Aden Arabie* (Boston: Beacon Press, 1960).

83 Fanon, *The Wretched of the Earth*, p. 58

84 Ibid.

85 Aimé Césaire, *The Tragedy of King Christophe* (New York: Grove Press, 1969), p. 13.

86 On this point see Michel Foucault, "The Ethic of Care for the Self as a Practice of Freedom," an interview translated by J. D. Gauthier, S. J., in *The Final Foucault*, ed. J. Bernauer and D. Rasmussen (Cambridge, Mass.: MIT Press, 1988), p. 3. As the reader will see, this basic and crucial theme of "the practice of freedom" and how it can possibly be established beyond the counter-violence directed against colonialism and neocolonialism will be the central focus of chapter 4.

87 Césaire, *The Tragedy of King Christophe*, p. 19.

88 Fanon, *The Wretched of the Earth*, p. 47.

89 Memmi, *The Colonizer and the Colonized*, pp. 51–66.

90 On this point see Memmi, *The Colonizer and the Colonized*, pp. 58–62. See also in this chapter note 7 and the related discussion of fascism and colonialism.

91 Fanon, *The Wretched of the Earth*, p. 60.

92 Memmi, *The Colonizer and the Colonized*, part two, the sections titled, "Mythical Portrait of the Colonized," and "Situations of the Colonized," *passim*.

93 On this point see Fanon's pioneering discussion in *Black Skin, White Masks*, chapter four, "The So-called Dependency Complex of Colonized Peoples." See also what Memmi calls "*The Usurper's Role* (or the Nero complex)," *The Colonizer and the Colonized*, pp. 52, 53.

94 See the second section of chapter 2.

95 See the first section of chapter 2.

96 The film, a 1968 production is based on Sembene's short novel, *The Money Order* (Portsmouth, N.H.: Heinemann Educational Books, 1988).

97 Fanon, *The Wretched of the Earth*, p. 150. On this point Sembene's novels and specifically *The Money Order* and *Xala* (Chicago: Lawrence Hill Books, 1976) are indispensable reading.

98 Taylor, *The Narrative of Liberation*, p. 10. As Taylor points out, for Fanon, neocolonialism and the domination of the liberation struggle, by the degenerate and counterfeit African "national bourgeoisie"—i.e., "Caliban become Prospero"—is the negative possibility that can develop (as indeed has happened in most of Africa) as a result of the failure of the African liberation struggle to concretely institutionalize its emancipatory possibilities. The obverse of this tragic situation is the as of yet unrealized possibility of concretely consolidating the gains of the African liberation struggle. This positive possibility, the desideratum of the African liberation struggle, will be the main focus of our discussion in chapter 4. For Fanon's pioneering discussion of this crucial point, see the section of *The Wretched of the Earth* titled, "The Pitfalls of National Consciousness."

99 I borrow this notion from Hans-Georg Gadamer, *Truth and Method* (New York: Crossroad Publishing Co., 1982), pp. 273–74. By the qualification "sociological" I mean only to suggest that, for me, "the fusion of horizons" is a concrete historical and ontic process that occurs in engaging real life issues and problems within the context of a specific historicalness. On the fundamental importance of this moment in the African liberation struggle, see Cabral, *Return to the Source: Selected Speeches*, p. 63.

100 Fanon, *The Wretched of the Earth*, p. 41.

101 Ibid., p. 146.

102 Ibid., p. 150.

103 On this point see chapter 1 in this study.

104 On this point, see Marx's third thesis in "Theses on Feuerbach," in Karl Marx and Frederick Engels, *The German Ideology* (New York: International Publishers, 1973), p. 121.

4. The Liberation Struggle

All emphasis in the original unless otherwise indicated.

1 Michel Foucault, "The Ethic of Care for the Self as a Practice of Freedom," an interview translated by J. D. Gauthier, S. J., in *The Final Foucault*, ed. J. Bernauer and D. Rasmussen (Cambridge, Mass.: MIT Press, 1988), p. 2.

2 Ibid., pp. 2–3, emphasis added.

3 Ibid., p. 4.

4 Ibid., p. 6.

5 Basil Davidson, *Africa in Modern History* (New York: Penguin Books, 1985), p. 374.

6 Michel Foucault, *Language, Counter-Memory, Practice* (Ithaca, N.Y.: Cornell University Press, 1977), p. 233. Foucault makes the above remark in a discussion with militant students in 1971, three years after May 1968. It should be noted that what Foucault affirms here was also affirmed long ago by Marx, against the utopian socialists.

7   Davidson, *Africa in Modern History*, part 6, section 32. To get a measure of Cabral's and the PAIGC's radical perspective, see Cabral's address at the CONCP (Confederation of the Nationalist Organizations of Portuguese Colonies) held in Dar-Es-Salaam in 1965: "The National Movements of the Portuguese Colonies," in *Revolution in Guinea: Selected Texts* (New York: Monthly Review Press, 1969). The other movement that Davidson mentions is the Eritrean People's Liberation Front (EPLF). After thirty years of struggle in which the EPLF was the leading armed movement, starting from the early 1970s, the Eritrean resistance won a complete political and military victory in May 1991.

8   Such an undertaking would require a study unto itself. Here I am only concerned with Cabral as an example of "the practice of freedom" in the context of the African liberation struggle. For more general discussions of Cabral, see Jock McCulloch, *In the Twilight of Revolution* (London: Routledge & Keagan Paul, 1983); and Patrick Chabal, *Amilcar Cabral* (New York: Cambridge University Press, 1983).

9   Frantz Fanon, *The Wretched of the Earth* (New York: Grove Press, 1968), p. 59, emphasis added.

10 Cornelius Castoriadis, *The Imaginary Institution of Society* (Cambridge, Mass.: MIT Press, 1987). In what follows I will argue that the process of African liberation is in fact a specific exemplification of the eruptive and magmatic process through which instituted or established societies (the colonial and neocolonial African status quo) are overcome by the self-institution of society out of the radical and foundational "imaginary" on which the African liberation struggle is grounded.

11 Fanon, *The Wretched of the Earth*, p. 124.

12 Leopold Sedar Senghor, *On African Socialism* (New York: Praeger, 1964), p. 81. In this regard, reflecting on his own political experience and practice, Kenneth David Kaunda makes the following very revealing remarks: "By 'rational' of course the white settlers meant the black opponent least likely to cause them anxiety or threaten their privileged position." Kenneth David Kaunda, *The Riddle of Violence* (New York: Harper & Row, 1980) p. 52.

13 Senghor, *On African Socialism*, p. 82. With Albert Memmi one needs to ask Senghor and his ilk: "How can one dare compare the advantages and disadvantages of colonization? What advantages . . . could make such internal and external catastrophes [i.e., the catastrophe of being colonized] acceptable?" *The Colonizer and the Colonized* (Boston: Beacon Press, 1967), p. 118.

14 Frantz Fanon, *Black Skin, White Masks* (New York: Grove Press, 1967), p. 12.

15 Franz Kafka, "A Report to an Academy," in *Selected Stories of Franz Kafka* (New York: Modern Library, 1952). The central character of Kafka's story—a humanized ape—is, to my mind, an apt example of the mentality and character of the unreformed Westernized African.

16 The portrayal of Westernized Africa presented by Sembene Ousmane in his films *Mandabi* (1969) and *Xala* (1974) are excellent examples of the character, or lack thereof, of this segment of contemporary African society. Being myself, to a limited extent, the offspring of this segment of African society, I can say from my own life experiences that Kafka's ape and Sembene's description are true to life in their characterizations.

17 Fanon, *The Wretched of the Earth*, p. 113.

18 Ibid.

19 Ibid.

20 Ibid., pp. 67–68.

21 Ibid., p. 68. The sentence as a whole reads: "This meeting of revolutionaries coming from the towns and country dwellers will be dealt with later on." This "later on" refers to the central idea of the *Wretched* which is the radical self-transformation of decolonized society such that the Westernized and non-Westernized native overcome their mutual self-estrangement and in their cultural-historical fusion institute and actualize the possibility of African self-emancipation. To be sure, the above is, in sum and very concisely, my reading of Fanon's politico-historical perspective.

22 On this point, see note 60 in this chapter.

23 Fanon, *The Wretched of the Earth*, p. 119.

24 Ibid., p. 127.

25 Ibid., p. 125.

26 Fanon, *Black Skin, White Masks*, p. 224.

27 I borrow the notion of originative history from Castoriadis's already cited work, *The Imaginary Institution of Society* (see note 10).

28 Friedrich Nietzsche, *On the Advantage and Disadvantage of History for Life* (Indianapolis: Hackett, 1980), p. 23.

29 In *The Imaginary Institution of Society*, Castoriadis develops this notion of history as a process of radical novelty in contradistinction to the tradition of European thought which basically sees history as a process of self-replication. On this point, please see specifically pp. 198, 272, and 343. On this point, see also Fanon's insightful remarks in *Black Skin, White Masks*, p. 229, and his call to inventiveness and creativity which concludes *The Wretched of the Earth*.

30 Fanon, *The Wretched of the Earth*, p. 147.

31 Ibid., pp. 153–54.

32 Ibid., pp. 164–66. It should be noted that Fanon was an opponent of the single-party state from its inception, when this self-serving idea was popular among many African leaders, who argued that to avoid ethnic/tribal conflict and to seriously engage in "development," single-minded government based on a single-party state was a necessity. Thirty years after the fact African popular opinion is beginning to appreciate, out of bitter experience, the critique of the single-party state articulated by Fanon in *The Wretched of the Earth*. On this point, please see Christopher Mulei, "Africa Needs Democracy," *New Africa*, no. 285 (June 1991), p. 26.

33 Fanon, *The Wretched of the Earth*, p. 176.

34 Ibid., p. 169.

35 For a detailed discussion of this central point in Fanon, which is seldom discussed in the literature on Fanon, please see *The Wretched of the Earth*, pp. 185–205. It should also be noted, as Fanon points out (p. 48), that the idea of mass popular democracy is not a novel idea in the context of Africa. Even in kingships and aristocratically ruled societies, problems of daily life, on the local level, have a tradition (on the whole) of being dealt with through the village assembly and in democratic deliberation among the elders and the responsible persons of the village.

In establishing peoples' assemblies, the liberation movements re-institute an old idea in a new context. Thus, the claim that Africa has no tradition of political democracy (on this point, see Ibrahim K. Sundiata, "The Roots of African Despotism: The Question of Political Culture," *African Studies Review*, vol. 31, no. 1 [April 1988]) is a rather bogus claim. One could say that it is limited by age and social standing, but in this respect even Athenian democracy—the pride of Europe!—was, one has to painfully remember, a democracy of slave masters which excluded women and the enslaved majority. Even contemporary Western democracies are not what they seem or appear to be. On this last point, please see Goran Therborn's classic paper, "The Rule of Capital and the Rise of Democracy," *New Left Review*, no. 103 (May–June 1977).

36   Fanon, *The Wretched of the Earth*, p. 194. It should be noted that the much abused word "republic" derives from the Latin *res publica*, which literally means the thing or affair of the people.

37   I am referring to Hannah Arendt's insightful remarks in chapter three of this study (note 73) which—in spite of her duplicity regarding the emancipatory efforts of non-European peoples—basically affirms what Fanon articulates regarding the possibilities of freedom created by the African liberation struggle.

38   Frantz Fanon, *Towards the African Revolution* (New York: Grove Press, 1988), p. 78. Over a period of ten years (circa 1974–1984) the Eritrean resistance repulsed ten such campaigns—comprising at any one time seventy to ninety thousand troops—while simultaneously instituting its democratic organs of popular mass democracy.

39   On this point, see also Karel Kosik, *Dialectics of the Concrete* (Dordrecht and Boston: D. Reidel Publishing Co., 1976), pp. 42–49.

40   Fanon, *The Wretched of the Earth*, pp. 126–27.

41   On this point please see chapter 3, section 2 of this study. It is imperative to note that Fanon was not merely a spectator or a "theorist" of social change. His writings are descriptive experiential narratives of the process of decolonization. In this sense one can say that Fanon is a phenomenologist of decolonization and his texts are documentations of this experience in the process of its unfolding.

42   Frantz Fanon, *A Dying Colonialism* (New York: Grove Press, 1965), see the first three chapters. It should be noted at this point that the fact that post-colonial Algeria regressed on many of its achievements and never achieved all that Fanon had hoped for does not in any way detract from the validity of Fanon's observations. As should be clear for anyone who has read his works, for Fanon the freedom and vitality of a people is something that has to be constantly struggled for and maintained. It cannot be achieved once and for all. Each generation has to actively hold on to the freedom it has inherited or forcefully reclaim the freedom that the previous generation failed to transmit to it.

43   See note 99 in chapter 3 of this study.

44   For a critical discussion of Gadamer's notion of "effective-historical consciousness," please see my paper, "Heidegger and Gadamer: Thinking as 'meditative' and as 'effective–historical Consciousness,' " *Man and World*, vol. 26, no. 1 (1987), pp. 59–61. For a more recent critical reading of Gadamer's notion of "effective-histori-

cal Consciousness," see Gail Soffer, "Gadamer, Hermeneutics, and Objectivity in Interpretation," *Praxis International*, vol. 12, no. 3 (October 1992).

45 Fanon, *Towards the African Revolution*, p. 34.

46 Ibid., p. 146

47 Ibid., p. 44.

48 Fanon, *The Wretched of the Earth*, p. 246, emphasis added. In contradiction to Fanon, Memmi asserts that: "We shall ultimately find ourselves before a counter mythology. . . . To hear the colonized . . . everything is good, everything must be retained among his customs and traditions, his actions and plans; even the anachronous or disorderly, the immoral or mistaken. Everything is justified because everything can be explained." *The Colonizer and the Colonized*, p. 139. In terms of his own depiction of the differing portraits and the possibilities of both the colonizer and the colonized, the above position seems to be completely untenable, precisely because it fails to take account of the dialectics of change that Memmi himself explores so well in the rest of his text. See also note 66 for Cabral's remarks on this point, which are in complete agreement with Fanon.

49 Fanon, *The Wretched of the Earth*, p. 216. As is well known, Fanon always thought through his reflections based on his own concrete experiences and observations in Martinique and in Europe and, more important, by focusing on the experiences of the Algerian Revolution and the then dynamic situation of Africa. In all of this Fanon utilizes to the maximum these limited historical experiences by theoretically exploring and unfolding the historical and dialectical necessities embedded in these concrete situations. As we have seen, this is why his reflections on the process of African self-emancipation or the present actualities of neocolonialism (thirty years ahead of time!) are so true to life. Indeed, Cabral's theoretic position concretely vindicates the depth and foresight of Fanon's much neglected work. As Pietro Clemente had noted (*Frantz Fanon, tra esistenzialismo e rivolutione*, Casa editrice Guis, Laterza & Figli, Bari Italia, via Dante 51) as early as 1971, the reason for this neglect in both Europe and Africa is the fact that Fanon makes—by the veracity of what he says—many people uncomfortable. On this point, see also Mrs. Josie Fanon, "His Solidarity Knew No National Boundaries," in *International Tribute to Frantz Fanon* (Record of the Special meeting of the United Nations Special Committee against Apartheid, 3 November 1978), p. 33.

50 Amilcar Cabral, *Revolution in Guinea: Selected Texts* (New York: Monthly Review Press, 1969), p. 76.

51 On this point, please see Mario de Andrade's biographical notes in *Unity and Struggle Speeches and Writings of Amilcar Cabral* (New York: Monthly Review Press, 1979).

52 Amilcar Cabral, *Return to the Source: Selected Speeches* (New York: Monthly Review Press, 1973), p. 63. The central point of the discussion to follow will be to explicate and detail the significance of this key formulation. It should be noted that Cabral places this phrase in inverted commas in order to differentiate himself from a merely personal and abstract—Pan-Africanism, Négritude, etc.—"return" to the African past or appropriation of it as a dead relic. On this point, see ibid., pp. 59–64.

53 Martin Heidegger, *What Is Philosophy?* (New Haven, Conn.: College & University Press, 1956), p. 97. Unlike Heidegger, however, Cabral is quite sanguine and consistent regarding the veracity of this view in his political involvements.

54 Cornelius Castoriadis, "The Greek Polis and the Creation of Democracy," *Graduate Faculty Philosophy Journal*, vol. 9, no. 2 (Fall 1983), p. 93.

55 Amilcar Cabral, *Revolution in Guinea: Selected Texts* (New York: Monthly Review Press, 1969), p. 76.

56 Amilcar Cabral, *Return to the Source*, p. 58

57 Ibid., p. 61.

58 Ibid.

59 This is also one of the central points that Fanon makes in *The Wretched of the Earth*, see the section titled, "On National Culture."

60 See Mario de Andrada's "Biographical Notes," in *Unity and Struggle: Speeches and Writings*, pp. xxvii–xxviii. See also the text and remarks in note 22 of this chapter. It should also be noted in this regard that initially, the Algerian struggle was a movement aimed not at independence but at obtaining equal rights—i.e., assimilation—for Algerians who, in the official propaganda of French colonialism, were supposed to be French citizens.

61 Cabral, *Return to the Source*, p. 62.

62 For an in-depth discussion of this historic/existential decision as a concrete possibility for human existence, please see Martin Heidegger, *Being and Time* (New York: Harper and Row, 1962) specifically section 74, p. 434.

63 Cabral, *Return to the Source*, p. 63.

64 Ibid., p. 63.

65 Ibid., p. 54.

66 Ibid., pp. 54–55.

67 Ibid., p. 55.

68 Ibid.

69 Ibid., p. 56.

70 On this point see Cabral's essay, "The Weapon of Theory," in *Revolution in Guinea*, specifically, p. 93. See also, *Our People Are Our Mountains*, Speeches of Amilcar Cabral, Collected by the British Committee for Freedom in Mozambique, Angola, and Guinea-Bissau (Nottingham, Eng.: Russell Press Ltd., 1971). Cabral describes the "ideology" of his movement thus: "Our desire to develop our country with social justice and power in the hands of the people is our ideological basis. Never again do we want to see a group or a class of people exploiting or dominating the work of our people. That's our basis. If you want to call it Marxism, you may call it Marxism. That's your responsibility. A journalist once asked me: "Mr. Cabral, are you a Marxist?" Is marxism a religion? I am a freedom fighter in my country. You must judge from what I do in practice. . . . But the labels are your affair; we don't like those kinds of labels" (p. 21). In other words, for Cabral, as for Fanon, in the context of the liberation struggle, theory is the concrete hermeneutic elucidation of the needs and requirements of the liberation struggle.

71 Cabral, *Revolution in Guinea, p. 102.*

72 Cabral, *Return to the Source*, p. 43.

73 Cabral, *Revolution in Guinea, p. 95.*

74 Ibid., p. 68.

75 Cabral, *Return to the Source*, p. 43.

76 Cabral, *Revolution in Guinea*, pp. 56–75.

77 Cabral, Return to the Source, p. 88, on this point see also note 70 in this chapter.

78 On this point, please see notes 70 and 77 in this chapter.

79 On this point see the concluding discussion of section 3 in chapter 1 of this study, starting from note 48. Please also note notes 50 and 53 in the indicated section of the first chapter.

80 Cabral, *Return to the Source*, p. 78. For interesting remarks on post-colonial Guinea-Bissau, see the preface by Basil Davidson to *No Fist is Big Enough to Hide the Sky* (London: Zed Books, 1984), pp. viii–xii. See also Basil Davidson, *The Fortunate Isles* (Trenton, N.J.: Africa World Press, 1989).

81 Fanon, *The Wretched of the Earth*, p. 311, emphasis added.

82 For a contrary perspective, see Cornelius Castoriadis, "Reflections on Racism," in *Thesis Eleven*, no. 32 (1992). The problem with Castoriadis's position is that it is incapable of making any meaningful distinctions between an aggressive and expansionist nationalism (i.e., of the right) and the nationalism of formerly colonized people, which stakes its claim to existence on the recognition of intercultural and interhistorical difference and solidarity. Eritrea, Guinea-Bissau, and post-1991 Ethiopia are, within the African context, the best examples of this kind of nationalism.

83 Aimé Césaire *Discourse on Colonialism* (New York: Monthly Review Press, 1972), p. 78.

84 Jean-Paul Sartre, introduction to *The Colonizer and the Colonized*, p. xxviii.

85 See note 50 in the first chapter of this study.

86 See the quotation given in note 53 in the first chapter of this study.

87 See the concluding discussion of chapter 1 starting from note 48 to the end of the chapter. See also Fanon, *The Wretched of the Earth*, p. 247.

88 For similar views on this point, see Kwasi Wiredu, "On Defining African Philosophy," p. 105; and Lansana Keita, "Contemporary African Philosophy: The Search for a Method," *passim*; both in *African Philosophy: The Essential Readings*.

89 Marcien Towa, "Propositions sur l'identitié culturelle," *Presence Africaine*, no. 109, 1st quarterly (1979), p. 87. The English version of this text is my own slightly altered rendering of a private translation by Dr. Victor Manfredi.

90 Ibid., pp. 84–85.

91 For the notion of philosophy as a hermeneutical inventory of one's lived historicity, which I borrow from Gramsci, see note 36 and the related discussion in chapter 1 of this study.

92 Michel Foucault, "The Ethic of Care for the Self as a Practice of Freedom," p. 20.

Conclusion

1 Hegel has perspicuously observed that, in philosophy, the end is and can only be the systematic recapitulation of the whole. In the *Phenomenology of Spirit*, for example, the section titled "Absolute Knowing," which is the apex and conclusion of the phenomenal manifestation and actualization of *Geist* is nothing more than a concise review of "the Science of knowing in the sphere of appearance." (Oxford: Oxford University Press, 1978), trans. A. V. Miller, paragraph 808, p. 493. In this regard, see also *Hegel's Philosophy of Right*, trans. T. M. Knox (Oxford: Oxford University Press, 1973), the addition to paragraph 256, the second paragraph to the addition on page 155.

2 Theophilus Okere, *African Philosophy. A Historico-Hermeneutical Investigation*, p. 124 (Lanham, MD: University Press of America, 1983).

3 Frantz Fanon, *Towards the African Revolution*, p. 44. (New York: Grove Press, 1988).

4 Outlaw, "African 'Philosophy': Deconstructive and Reconstructive Challenges," in *Contemporary Philosophy: A New Survey*, vol. 5, African Philosophy, p. 11. ed., Guttom Floistad (Dordrecht, Netherlands: Martinus Nijhoff, 1987).

5 Ngugi wa Thiong'o, *Decolonizing the Mind* (Portsmouth, N.H.: Heinemann Educational Books, 1987). It cannot be emphasized enough that the phrase "return to the source" is *not* meant to suggest a "return" to a primordial "truth" or some uncontaminated "African *arche*." As we saw in chapter 4, what is to be returned to and appropriated is the vigor and actuality of African existence which is reawakened by the liberation struggle. In other words, it is the reignited historicity of African existence that is the "source" to which the "return" is directed by the exigencies of the liberation struggle.

6 Edward Said, *Orientalism* (New York: Vintage Books, 1979), p. 272.

7 Kwame Anthony Appiah, "Is the Post- in Postmodernism the Post- in Postcolonial?" *Critical Inquiry*, vol. 17, no. 2 (Winter 1991).

8 Cheikh Hamidou Kane, *Ambiguous Adventure*, p. 73. (Portsmouth NH: Heinemann Educational Books, 1989)

Index